THE WRECK
OF THE BARQUE
Stefano

THE WRECK
OF THE BARQUE

Stefano

OFF THE NORTH WEST
CAPE OF AUSTRALIA
IN 1875

GUSTAVE RATHE

FARRAR, STRAUS & GIROUX

NEW YORK

For my mother
EUXENIA BACCICH RATHE
born on the fifteenth anniversary
of the
wreck of the barque *Stefano*
October 27, 1890
died April 7, 1978

CONTENTS

LIST OF ILLUSTRATIONS

FOREWORD

Although the title suggests otherwise, this book is not so much about a shipwreck as about castaways. The story of the sudden grounding of the *Stefano* and its quick destruction is quickly told in a few pages. The greater part of the book is about the hard life led by the castaways in a then remote part of northwestern Australia before the last two survivors—two youths—were rescued, with the help of local Aborigines, six months later, in April 1876.

As such, this book belongs to collections about castaways, which have a literature of their own, for accounts of castaways and the marooned, even more than shipwrecks, have the stuff for good stories and dramas, both tragic and comic.

English literature is replete with such stories—Shakespeare's drama about the adventures of Prospero and his fellow castaways on Caliban's enchanted island in the West Indies told in *The Tempest*, Daniel Defoe's biography of *Robinson Crusoe*, Robert Louis Stevenson's *Treasure Island*, R. M. Ballantyne's *Coral Island*, Jonathan Swift's *Gulliver's Travels*, and Rudyard Kipling's *Captains Courageous*, where he tells the story of young Harvey Cheyne, to mention but a few.

Some of these stories are romantic accounts about exotic lands, such as Prospero's enchanted island where life can be lived effortlessly in a "golden land" well bequeathed by nature, rather like those Andrew Marvell describes in his poem "Bermudas" and in other verses. Other accounts are of castaways in harsh lands like Herman Melville's "Encantadas," which were "disowned by man and wolf alike" and "refused to harbour even the outcasts of beasts."

This story is of the latter type, about some castaways' struggle to exist in a harsh land with little water and not much food to gather after their own food supplies ran out, and this is what makes the book unique and interesting. It describes the north-western region of Australia from Exmouth Gulf down to near Red Bluff, that is, much of the present Ningaloo area in its pristine state, as seen through the eyes of two young Croatian boys. It also tells of the fine sea tradition of the islanders of the Adriatic, whose contribution to maritime history is equal to that of the noted Åland Islanders of the Baltic, famous for their tall ships. Most significantly, it provides an account of the Aboriginal tribes who helped save and sustain the two young lads, and arranged to have them rescued. Such accounts are rare in Western Australian history, and so the publication of this one is most welcome.

Leslie R. Marchant,
B.A. Hons. (W.A.), M.A. (Lond.), F.R.G.S.
Associate Professor of History,
University of Western Australia

INTRODUCTION

The last quarter of the nineteenth century saw the demise of the great ships of sail. Yet, during that period of decline, there were more than 1,800 shipwrecks in Australia's coastal waters!

This is a remarkably high figure when one considers the relatively small population of Australia and the level of the country's economic activity during that period. It is startling to consider the great loss of lives that must have resulted from the tragedies. There is no doubt that ocean travel was hazardous a hundred years ago, even though newspapers of the period often gave rather brief and bland accounts of the wrecks. Media interest was highest when a disaster was costly in human lives, but little seems to have been written that reflects the human drama: the terror, the struggle for survival, and the personal reactions of those involved.

My study of news accounts has given me the impression that wrecks which occurred in the waters off the more populous southeastern coast of Australia were more likely to benefit from rescue efforts, while wrecks which occurred along the uninhabited coasts often proved really tragic. The majority of maritime disasters involved ships engaged in the Australian coastal trade, though there was also a considerable amount of international traffic in the oceans of the region: Dutch ships developing a lucrative trade with the East Indies, Yankee whaling ships, and British vessels engaged in the China trade.

It was in the loss of these international ships that we especially sense some of the high drama of shipwreck and the fears the seamen would have had about perishing somewhere along the vast stretches of uninhabited shores. The west coast of Australia was the scene of many early wrecks, since it was the part of the continent first sighted by European ships bound for the Orient or the South Pacific on voyages of colonization and trade. The *Batavia* is the best known of several Dutch vessels of pre-settlement times that have been designated wrecks of historical significance by the Western Australian government. Some distance north of the *Batavia*'s graveyard, the American ship *Rapid*, out of Boston, went down at Point Cloates in 1811. The dramatic uncovering of that ship's identity and the reconstruction of her story are a credit to the maritime archaeologists and the Western Australian Museum. The *Batavia* meets one of the criteria of a historic wreck: significance to early Australian history. The *Rapid* meets another: some hint of adventure, intrigue, or riches associated with the ship.

The *Stefano* does not meet the usual criteria for being designated a wreck of historic significance. The ship was of Austro-Hungarian registry. But this tells us only that political control of its home port was in the hands of the Habsburgs at that time. There was not a single Austrian or Hungarian on board; most, if not all, of the crew would have regarded themselves as Dalmatians. In 1875, the dual monarchy of Austria-Hungary embraced the eastern Adriatic coastline from Trieste in the north to the Bay of Kotor in the south.

The inhabitants of the Dalmatian littoral had dominated the maritime trade of the Mediterranean during the sixteenth and seventeenth centuries. Their prowess was not widely known outside the region, although several of Dubrovnik's ships were impressed into the Spanish Armada for its disastrous foray against England in 1588. Vessels from the republic of Venice and the city-states of Dubrovnik and Korčula were frequently chartered by the British in later times to support the commerce of their empire.

The crews who manned the ships were from families who had successfully toiled on the sea for more than three hundred years. In fact, the maritime trade had begun as early as the tenth century, when Mislav, son of Tomislav, the first King of Croatia, was given control of a settlement at a middle point of the Dalmatian coast.

In the course of some five centuries, overpopulation, overgrazing, and overplanting had between them damaged the fragile countryside in the district near Diocletian's palace (now the city of Split). Mislav, evidently troubled about the condition of the land, took bold but sensible steps to lead his countrymen toward a more promising future. He resettled on a large island about fifty miles away in the Adriatic Sea. The island—Corcyra Nigra, later named Korčula—had been sparsely settled by the Illyrians, Greeks, and Romans centuries before, but was virtually uninhabited when Mislav arrived with his fellow colonists. Early records give strong evidence that they succeeded in establishing a substantial and successful maritime industry by the sixteenth century.[1] They not only built oceangoing sailing ships at Korčula but also manned them and followed the principal trade routes of the world.

Toward the end of the nineteenth century, this way of life gradually came to a halt as ships of iron powered by steam engines took over the trade. Lacking the natural resources of iron ore and coal, Dalmatia could not make the transition, and Britain and Germany became the leaders in European shipbuilding.

The first and last voyage of the *Stefano* occurred during this
time of change. Thanks to the two survivors, my grandfather
Miho Baccich and his shipmate Ivan Jurich, we have a detailed
account of what was a commonplace occurrence—the calamity of
shipwreck.

This book is an adaptation of the account of the adventure
recorded by Father Stjepan Skurla, S.J., who had many conversations with the two young survivors in 1876, a year after the
wreck but only a few months following the rescue. I have added
information obtained in interviews with Baccich's family and with
the descendants of Captain Charles Tuckey, the rescuer. I visited
Australia, located the site of the wreck, using a map drawn by
Baccich, and gathered more information as I retraced most of the
journey of the young castaways.

Baccich and Jurich both had a gift for remembering details.
They had ample opportunity to recall and record many of their
experiences after their rescue, even before their return to Dubrovnik. Skurla made at least two copies of the story related to
him. He wrote the original account in Italian,* the local language
of commerce and record at that time. It was not until 1920 that
Baccich's wife completed a translation into English. I first read
the story in about 1930, when I lived with my grandfather for a
time. My interest in the adventure grew stronger as the years
went by. During the early part of World War II, I served with
Australians in the South Pacific and entertained hopes of getting
to Australia to visit the scenes of the story, but I was transferred
back to the United States without having an opportunity to do
so.

Repeated notions of visiting the scene were thwarted by the
remoteness of the North West Cape—there seemed to be no
settlements, no good roads anywhere near where I wanted to go.
Many years slipped by. Then, in 1965, I came across a newspaper
account referring to a U.S. Navy installation on the North West
Cape of Australia in the center of the area I wanted to explore.
When I wrote to the Navy, I learned that good roads and accom-
modations now existed in the area. Even with this encouraging
information, I procrastinated until a newfound friend in Tasmania,

---

* Its title is *I naufraghi del bark austro-ungarico "Stefano" alla costa Nord-
Ouest dell'Australia.*

I naufraghi del bark austro-ungarico
„Stefano"
alla costa Nord-Ovest dell'Australia

I

Era il dì 31 luglio 1875,
quando il bark austro-ungarico „Stefano" lasciata la rada
di Cardiff, e per 60 miglia ri-
morchiato da un battello a
vapore fino all'isola di Lan-
dy, abbandonava la costa in-
glese, sciogliendo le vele al ven-
to per darsi all'alto mare.
I marinai, esperti nella
manovra, fornirono ben presto
l'albero di prora del suo trin-
chetto, parrocchetto, pappafico, e
contrappappafico; quello di maestra, delle vele maestra, gabbie,
pappafico di maestra, e contra.

*First page of the original manuscript, handwritten in Italian
by Stjepan Skurla, S.J., 1876, Dubrovnik, Croatia*

F. Murray Arthur, M.D., succeeded in getting me to take some action. More than that, he began a search for Captain Tuckey's descendants by placing an advertisement in the Perth newspapers. When he received numerous replies, he sent the information on to me. This led to my meeting John Honniball of Perth, the captain's great-grandson, a Fellow of the Royal Western Australian Historical Society, and the author of a published family history that included an account of the wreck of the Stefano[2] based on early newspaper accounts. It is Jack Honniball to whom I am most indebted for helping me complete this book. Apart from giving me his own suggestions and records, he introduced me to several members of the Tuckey family, who in turn contributed recollections, letters, and photographs to my efforts. I was also introduced to another rich source of information, Neven Smoje of Perth. He and his wife, Jeanette, have become my good friends. Of Croatian descent himself, Neven had also written an article about the wreck of the Stefano.[3] His work was based on the duplicate copy of the manuscript, which he searched out in Rijeka, and translated into English. With unlimited generosity, he turned all of his material, with sources and photographs, over to me and provided introductions to his friends in Croatia, who later helped me gather more data.

The task of organizing such varied material was quite complex. The story began as an oral history related by teenagers in Croatian, was recorded by a scholar in Italian, and was translated into English half a century later—and all had to be restated in clear modern prose and combined appropriately with the new source material. This challenging requirement was met by Karleen Redle, who edited, organized, and reedited everything I produced.

In the course of publication, it proved desirable to make some changes in the general construction and to insert further material. This work needed to be done in Western Australia, close to the new source material. Jack Honniball and Neven Smoje kindly accepted the delegated task, and their many contributions to the final product have added much to its accuracy, comprehensibility, and quality.

I must also thank many others for their special contributions to this work: Mr. Nenad Gol of Zagreb, who had published a brief account of the Stefano shipwreck in Croatian; Dr. Professor Josip Luetić, curator of the maritime museum in Dubrovnik, who gave me an understanding of the place in history achieved by the maritime fleets of Dalmatia; and Dr. Milos Vujnovich of New Orleans, professor and author, who encouraged me in many ways and provided me with important material about Baccich. Also, I thank Father Don Ivo Protic, parish priest in Blato, Korčula, who traced Baccich's roots back to the sixteenth- and seventeenth-century mariners of the Adriatic. Special gratitude goes to Admiral Marko Ohranovich, who served in the Yugoslav Navy during World War II, and who helped me find what became of Ivan Jurich, the co-survivor of the shipwreck.

Others to whom I give my appreciation include the late Edgar Lefroy, Mrs. Billie Lefroy, and daughter Jane of Ningaloo Station, which overlooks the site of the shipwreck; the Australian Embassy in Washington, D.C.; the U.S. Navy facility at Exmouth, Western Australia; Ivana Burdelez of the government archives in Dubrovnik; Peter Bridge; Leslie Marchant; Monica Vincent; Fay Heath; Kay Carlson; and Greg Rathe, cameraman.

Finally, I am thankful for the wonderful factotum who typed, filed, edited, retyped, mailed, proofread, traveled, advised, promoted, corrected, inspired, and endured—my wife, Lesslie.

Gustave Rathe

The coast, from the moment we first saw it, exhibited nothing but a picture of desolation; no rivulet consoled the eye; no tree attracted it; no mountain gave variety to the landscape; no dwelling enlivened it; everywhere reigned sterility and death.

—A description of the west coast of
Australia written by the French artist
Jacques Etienne Victor Arago at Shark
Bay, Western Australia, 1818[1]

THE WRECK
OF THE BARQUE
Stefano

I

Outward Bound

My mother was too cheerful. I suspected that she was really sad and, perhaps, worried, although there was no need for her to feel that way. On both sides of the family there had been many sea captains. Her father-in-law, whom she knew well, was Anton Bacetich.* He was from Korčula, an island only forty miles from Dubrovnik, and the birthplace of many world travelers, including (so they say there) Marco Polo. My grandfather owned several oceangoing ships and he had sailed all over the world.

The ship that I was to sail on the next day was exceptionally fine. My uncle Nikola Baccich had had the *Stefano* built in Rijeka that year. It was superb! Nearly 1,000 tons, 160 feet over all—twice as large as the average barque. Each of the sixteen men in the crew had deep-water experience. Miloslavich, the captain, was my first cousin, and the others were close friends.

To me it seemed inevitable that my life's work would be at sea. This was my nation's work; we had one of the largest and best merchant fleets in the world. Unlike the warships of Great Britain, France, and Spain, or the whaling ships with their dangerous work sailing uncharted seas, our ships sailed the established trade routes on missions of peace that I associated with progress.

I reminded my mother of all this in hopes of cheering her up.

* Bacetich is a diminutive form of Baccich.

Cadet Miho Baccich,
1875, age sixteen

Captain Vlaho Miloslavich,
1875, age twenty-six

Deputy Captain Karlo
Costa, 1875, age twenty-four

Although she listened attentively, she didn't seem to understand and she responded to just part of what I had said.

"You are all so young. Your captain is only twenty-six and he's the oldest among you. You're barely sixteen. You're just a bunch of boys going halfway round the world to trade with strangers!" And that was all she said.

By the end of the next day we were sailing the Adriatic and the Mediterranean for Cardiff, Wales, to take on the *Stefano*'s cargo—1,300 tons of coal for delivery to Hong Kong. During the short voyage I was exhilarated and I knew my shipmates were, too. Although I knew I was carrying on a family tradition, it was the sheer adventure of going to sea that had made me so eager to leave home.

In Cardiff, all of us became impatient as the dirty coal was loaded into our new, clean ship. Shortly before we were towed to sea on the last day of July 1875, the captain brought a young English boy on board. Harry Groiss† (that was his name) couldn't have been more than ten or eleven years old, but he was to be our cabin boy. I couldn't see why we needed one, and I wondered how his parents could let him go. Perhaps he was an orphan or was running away. Worrying about him made me realize why my mother had been concerned about my going to sea.

The next day we cast off from the towing launch near Lundy Island, some sixty miles from Cardiff, and our sails were unfurled for the four-month, 15,000-mile journey. I hadn't the slightest concern about our journey or any idea that we wouldn't return safely. I certainly had no premonition that Harry Groiss would perish.

The *Stefano* sailed southward on the customary route in the Atlantic, and soon passed the Azores and the Madeira island groups. Sailing west of the Canary Islands, we saw the 12,000-foot peak of Tenerife in the distance, and we soon crossed the Tropic of Cancer. I can't remember any details of those pleasant days in the tropical Atlantic. The events that occurred later must have blotted them out.

I do, however, recall crossing the equator. There were the customary celebrations for first-time voyagers. I also remember the excitement of our first encounter with another vessel after leaving

---

† The name Groiss is probably a corruption of Grice or Grose.

England. Such an encounter is called "speaking a ship." Each ship "backs" about half of her sails to stay motionless and extend the period of contact in order to exchange information and greetings. This has a distinct effect on one's emotions. Although strangers, all feel the common bond of occupation and a temporary release from loneliness.

The most memorable event of that first leg of our voyage occurred after we rounded the stormy Cape of Good Hope, so inappropriately named by John II of Portugal. It was the first of September and we were thirty-two days out of Cardiff when a terrible storm beset us. On the following day the wind worsened until it was necessary to shorten sail. All of us took our turns aloft. Fatigue and constant danger changed our previous happy adventure to an experience of discomfort and a recognition of possible peril.

All sails but two lower topsails and the jib were furled. Even so, the wind, seemingly determined to offset the slight advantage we gained, increased in fury. The wind whistling in the shrouds and the halyards and sheets rattling as they slapped against the spars created a frightening clamor. The barque pitched and rolled and seemed to disappear entirely when the towering waves struck. At times the crests ahead seemed so immense that I doubted the ship could mount any of them. As the ship raced down the following troughs, it would stall with a shudder, and the rolling and pitching increased until the ends of the yards touched the water. It was impossible to stay on your feet. We would have lost several men overboard if we hadn't had stout lifelines rigged fore and aft. I recalled a painting at home: two men lashed to the wheel of a storm-tossed craft so they wouldn't be washed overboard. The scene appeared to come to life when I glanced aft and saw both helmsmen similarly bound to their post. The painting hadn't exaggerated the drama of a storm at sea.

On the ninth day the storm finally abated. We must have been moving with it across the Indian Ocean because, even with only two sails set, we had covered about three hundred miles.

The days that followed were beautiful enough to repay us for the ugly weather we had been through. How quickly we forgot the painful past, and how readily we enjoyed the present without giving a thought to the future. But I did think about the experience as the first test of my vocation to a life at sea; and although I knew that at that very moment, in one ocean or another, equally terrified men were enduring the kind of storms we had survived, I knew I was willing to undergo such tempests again and again to be one of that company who follow the sea.

Our next landfall was to be the uninhabited island of St. Paul. The tiny dot in the middle of the southern Indian Ocean was used by navigators from all lands to set their chronometers and to compare their sextant sights with the known latitude and longitude of this station. We were now about twenty-five days from the Cape of Good Hope and had logged a distance of 2,900 miles. Because of the clouds and heavy fog, we were not able to verify our instruments or establish a precise course. This didn't bother us because we figured we were only twenty days from the west coast of Australia, where we would have another opportunity to sight land from far enough offshore to check our instruments, plot our position, and chart a route up the coast, after which we would head for the East Indies, going through the eastern passage to enter the Pacific Ocean through the Ombai Strait. Then we would sail south of the Philippines and on to Hong Kong.

The prevailing west wind favored us, and although the ocean was a little rough, conditions were ideal. The ship maintained a speed of about twelve knots, and as we neared the coast of Australia, the wind shifted southerly, providing favorable conditions for us to turn northward.

At noon on October 26, we could see the coast of Australia from the topmast. In less than one month we had covered the 2,200 miles from St. Paul. In another month, with good weather, we should be in Hong Kong, our destination. Thoughts of the voyage home were already with us.

Because of possible coral reefs and submerged rocks along the incompletely charted coast, the captain decided to set our course west of north, keeping the *Stefano* well offshore until we should pass the North West Cape. By nightfall we crossed the Tropic of Capricorn for the second time, this time in a northwesterly direction; the crew members who were off duty retired for the night, while the others remained on deck to finish their watch.

2

Shipwreck

At the stroke of midnight on October 26/27, the first mate, Martin Osojnak, the quartermaster, Bucich, and Perancich, Dediol, Vulovich, Brajevich, and Antoncich were on watch. About 2 a.m., Osojnak came below for a cup of coffee and stayed for a few moments talking with Jurich, who was preparing for the next watch. I was in my bunk, not too far away, half-awake. The mate had barely returned to his post when the ship's bell sounded 2:30 a.m., and at the same moment the ship gave a violent lurch to starboard—shaking, grinding, then abruptly coming to a halt. In another second, all was silent. The *Stefano* had grounded on a submerged rock or hidden coral reef.

The sudden violence of the shock made us realize immediately what had happened, and all of us below scrambled on deck in panic. Though aground, the vessel still pitched and rolled, each wave pounding it furiously on the rocks. The awful grinding noise, together with the violent shivering of the spars, increased our terror.

Captain Miloslavich ordered more sails set in hopes that the strong wind and intermittent swells would right the ship and raise us from the rocky depths. The wind was now at gale force, and the merciless pounding increased. The sounding rod showed no deep water on either side of the stricken ship, and the hull was almost filled with water. We rushed to the pumps to discharge our watery ballast but were disappointed: the pumps would not work. The order was given to abandon ship, using any small boats that could be launched. Several men went below to gather whatever food, water, and tools might be salvaged from the flooding cabins. The rest of us tried to launch the lifeboats. The task proved more than we could handle because the lines and blocks had become hopelessly tangled by the motion of the *Stefano* as she pounded and pitched against the rocks. I was too busy helping with the lifeboats to realize we would probably drown and worried about only one minute at a time.

There were few moments to lose, and had it not been for the courage and superhuman strength of Perancich, who managed to climb up the mast and out on a yardarm to untangle the blocks and lines, we would not have been able to launch the small boats. The first yawl ready for launching was filled with the casks of fresh water, provisions, and clothing. Following the rules of the sea, we placed the young English boy, Harry Groiss, in it. All the elements were working against us; the boat had hardly been lowered in its blocks when a towering wave crashed across the main deck. In an instant the gigantic wall of water lifted the yawl with its precious cargo, then dashed it with tremendous force against the side of the ship. The single wave smashed the boat to pieces and the poor English boy was crushed by the shattered timbers. We watched helplessly as he was quickly swept from view amid the tangle of wood, shredded sails, and lines that clogged the water in the lee of the ship. It was only then that we really wondered about him—where he had come from and how we could ever tell his mother what had happened.

But the water that washed over the deck swept Harry Groiss from our thoughts when Perancich, who had climbed the rigging to help launch the boat, was carried overboard. Clinging desperately to the spar on which he had been working, he quickly disappeared, too. It now seemed hopeless; there was no longer any chance of using the remaining lifeboats if we couldn't even get near them. There had been some order and sense of purpose before; now all was chaos, every man for himself.

Antoncich was the first to act. He grabbed a cabin ladder about six feet long and jumped into the sea from the higher, leeward side of the broken ship. This struck me as the best thing to do, so I grabbed a ladder and jumped, as did Costa, the deputy captain. Just as we joined Antoncich in the water, an unrecognizable shipmate shouted to us from the high side of the ship, "Courage, my brothers, farewell!" As his words broke the awful silence of the water beyond the ship, another murderous wave struck and hurled him to eternity.

By now I knew that the ladder, my would-be life raft, was a mistake. It barely kept me afloat, and it actually hindered me as I tried to move toward the shore, which I reckoned to be nearly ten miles east. So I decided to return to the ship while I still could. By the time I reached it, the wind and water had driven it farther aground. It was now higher in the water but still on its side. Because it was rocking less, it looked safer than when I had left it just a short while ago.

I realized the ship had been turned around 180° so that the bow was facing south. The underside of the ship offered some protection from the impact of the waves, but it was too sheer for me to climb. Tiring quickly, I was becoming desperate. There was no help to be had from those who had remained on board. Then Providence came to my aid, the first of many such occasions when I would receive unanticipated assistance. As I trod water in the lee of the hull, a large swell carried me high above the waterline and raised me enough that I could catch hold of an iron fastening that projected from the exposed side of the ship. I climbed over the side and found myself again among companions.

Seeing me, they seemed to realize survival was possible. Because the ship now had a more solid purchase on the rock, they had succeeded in reaching another lifeboat. They had already loaded this boat with some nautical instruments and provisions, and they were about to launch it from the now-stable wreckage. Four of us—Captain Miloslavich, Osojnak, Bucich, and I—worked at the task. Three other shipmates—the second mate, Lovrinovich; Zanetovich; and Vulovich—huddled in the safety of the forepeak. Pavisich, Radovich, Jurich, and Brajevich were perched in the highest rigging of the remaining mast. They decided to stay with the ship rather than come with us in the boat.

I suspected that whoever hailed me when I jumped over the side had probably perished with Harry Groiss and Perancich. Costa and Antoncich, I assumed, were still afloat on their ladders. That meant only three were unaccounted for. I prayed they were still safe.

Miraculously, the four of us launched the boat, and the next

wave carried us safely away from the wreck. But the eddy from the wave broached the boat about fifty yards from the ship and swamped us.

By grasping the keel of the overturned boat, I was able to surface. The others seemed to have been engulfed in the dark ocean. Hardly had I realized how tenuous my safety was when I saw a shipmate struggling in the water. It was Dediol. With the help of a life preserver, he managed to reach the overturned yawl and grabbed hold. Our combined efforts—his at the bow, mine at the stern—enabled us to right the boat and climb aboard. The water was up to the gunwale and we had nothing to bail with. The boat was often awash and we were barely able to keep it afloat. Still, it was a welcome haven. Our feeling of security did not last long; a heavy swell capsized us a second time. Yet again, with painful exertion, we righted the boat.

Later I learned that Bucich had survived the first swamping shortly after we had successfully launched the lifeboat. Clinging to some large wreckage, he had witnessed Captain Miloslavich and first mate Osojnak struggle and drown. Bucich managed to get back to the ship and the seven shipmates still on board. They huddled together in the shrouds until daybreak, when the mainmast fell. They realized they could not stay on the ship any longer; it was about to break up. One by one they climbed the foremast, eased along a yardarm, and leaped into the water, hoping to find floating wreckage to use to get to shore. Three of them—Bucich, Lovrinovich, and Jurich—struggled all day. Four others—Radovich, Zanetovich, Vukasinovich, and Pavisich—drowned after abandoning ship. No one could account for Brajevich.

For six long hours we struggled toward shore. The mental anguish was worse than the painful fatigue of keeping the small boat right side up and moving. It didn't seem as if we were getting any closer to land. But slowly the clouds began to drift away and the light of the morning star, followed by the false dawn, encouraged us. We had covered about half the distance. The land looked closer. Suddenly I saw a sail! Hope rose in our hearts, and although our throats were parched, we shouted and yelled for almost an hour. The suspense was tantalizing but our hopes were again crushed. It was only a small raft of wreckage manned by one of our ship's crew. He had found a large white board and upended it to help him move with the wind. This was the "sail"!

Even so, we were happy that Costa, who had entered the water with Antoncich and me, had managed to survive. He abandoned the raft and joined us in our sinking boat, which now had a hole in the bottom from striking a reef we had passed. The three of us felt sure we could make it to land, which seemed to be only three or four miles away. We had clear water ahead and a favorable wind and current astern. We were too numb from physical pain and mental apprehension to do more than drift. We didn't speak. I thought about what had happened and the toll it had taken of our small crew.

At 2 p.m., about twelve hours after the shipwreck, we washed ashore, barely breathing and fully exhausted. An hour later, Lovrinovich, Antoncich, and Bucich drifted to shore, clinging to flotsam from the stricken ship. Toward sundown, Jurich arrived alone, having swum most of the way.

The only comfort we could give to the worst-off—Antoncich, who was naked—was to cover him with some of our own clothes. One by one, we crawled farther from the water and, with our aching hands, dug burrows in the warm, dry sand. We spent the first night under the sand and gave no thought to tomorrow.

The following roster of the ship's crew as listed in the original manuscript gives their names in Croatian, their respective home-towns, and their posts aboard ship:

Vlaho Miloslavić	Dubrovnik	Captain
Karlo Costa	Dubrovnik	Deputy captain
Martin Osojnak	Rijeka	First mate
Ivan Lovrinović	Dubrovnik	Second mate
Domenic Antoncić	Mali Lošinj	Ship's carpenter
Miho Bacić	Dubrovnik	Cadet or midshipman
Mato Zanetović	Kotor	Cook
Baldassare Vukasinović	Gruž	
Josip Perancić	Mali Lošinj	
Grego Pavisić	Rijeka	Quartermaster
Fortuna Bucić	Rijeka	Quartermaster

Ivan Pavlo Radović	Potomje	
Ivan Jurić	Oskorušno	
Toma Dediol	Kućište	
Bozidar Vulović	Dobrota	
Nicola Brajević	Konavli	
Henry Groiss	Cardiff, Wales	Cabin boy

3

On the Beach

Hardly had the following day (October 28) dawned when we unfortunates, strengthened somewhat by the night's rest, gathered to search for possible wreckage or provisions which might have been washed ashore. Foremost in our wishes was the hope that we would find other survivors. A quick comparison of our individual experiences on the preceding day revealed that seven companions were known, or thought, to have perished. In order, they were Henry Groiss, the cabin boy; Miloslavich, the captain; Osojnak, the first mate; Zanetovich, the cook; and Vukasinovich, Pavisich, and Radovich.

Ashore now, besides myself, were Costa and Dediol, who had been with me in the half-sunken dinghy, and Lovrinovich, Antoncich, Bucich, and Jurich, who swam most of the way. With seven believed dead and seven together on shore, there were still three unaccounted for: Perancich, Brajevich, and Vulovich. We knew Perancich had been swept from the rigging after the fatal launching of the first lifeboat. The other two, who had jumped into the water from the main mast with no life preservers, were among the last to abandon ship.

We decided to walk north along the beach because the wind had shifted to south of west. We saw a large point of land jutting out into the ocean a mile or two north—a barrier that might catch any floating material blown in that direction by the wind.

The offshore reef appeared to parallel the coast and seemed to be about three or four miles out. This suggested that the *Stefano* had not struck a reef, or at least not the major reef which we could see breaking from shore. It must have struck submerged rocks [Point A on the map in the color insert, following page 74].

Even in early morning at this latitude, the sand was uncomfortably hot to my bare feet. Though the beach was wide and sandy, with no rocks, we left Jurich behind because he had a badly injured foot and could hardly walk. We could see beach grass and dunes beyond the sand. There was very little surf because the offshore reef broke the force of the waves before they reached land.

About half a mile north, we rushed ahead when we saw what appeared to be a body face down in the sand at the very edge of the water. It was Brajevich, still breathing but injured and barely conscious. We could not get him on his feet and were too weary to carry him. So we dragged him farther up onto dry, warm sand, covered him as best we could, and continued our search for something from the wreckage that might help us. We had gone only half a mile when we were rewarded. We found a lot of wreckage along a point extending to the north and west [Point Cloates, near Point O on the map]. There were two cases of wine, a barrel of flour, a large can of lard, a barrel of beans, some olive oil and other canned goods, meat, barrels of onions and potatoes, and other foodstuffs. Most we just moved above the high-water mark so it wouldn't be washed away by the tide. We opened a bottle of wine, rationed portions for ourselves, and kept some to take to Brajevich and Jurich.

A cry from Costa alerted us to something else on the beach ahead. It looked like another body and, indeed, was Vulovich, huddled motionless as if awaiting death. Like Brajevich, he was unable to stand, but we were able to revive him with the wine and half dragged, half carried him back to where we had left Brajevich. Brajevich also responded to the wine and, with help, was able to accompany us when we returned to our point of departure. There were nine of us now and only Perancich had not been accounted for.

We celebrated by having our first meal—small crabs and crayfish that we gathered from the beach at low tide. We shelled them and rolled them in a paste of wine and flour. Even uncooked, they were quite good and improved our condition so much that all of us were able to walk along the point to look for more supplies that might have washed ashore beyond where our previous sortie had taken us. Providence again favored us; we found the most important treasure of all, a cask of water, which all of us sorely needed. Farther on, there were two kegs of wine, and, just a few steps from the cask, the body of Radovich, who we had already concluded was dead.

In the scorching sun the body was beginning to decay, so with our hands we dug a shallow grave in the soft sand only yards from where the body lay, just where the sand met the sparse dune vegetation. When the last handful of sand was placed on top of the grave, Costa spoke these words for Radovich and those who had perished in the water:

Dear God:
Last night a robust crew of youth stormed heaven
And in their midst a fair-haired child—
His face and pleading eyes still haunt me—
None tired by life's long journey, all fit to serve You well.
Keep them together if only to comfort those they left behind,
Who know that union with one another
Is closest to union with You. Amen!

The condition of Radovich's corpse had made it obvious that the climate was a double peril. The sun was unbearable during the day, and the night had been damp and chilly. So we hurried to collect as much wreckage as we could find. We spent the rest of the day erecting a shelter. We found hatch covers, the pilot wheel, ladders, tables, empty boxes and casks, the boatswain's trunk, parts of lifeboats, and sections of masts, yards, and oars. The chest still contained two coats, three shirts, a needle and some thread, two carpenter's planes, and about twenty yards of cotton cloth, of great value to us ill-clothed survivors. There was also a packet of letters from the ship's owner to the deceased captain, Miloslavich.

We began building a camp a short distance from the sea, where we had washed ashore. It was a sandy plain with small patches

Campsite area, Camp Hill

of grassy growth [Point B on the map]. It looked as if part of it was the bed of a dry stream. On the south side of the clearing was a very high hill which protected us from the southerly sea breeze.‡ To the northwest we looked down on a grassy plain with a few small shrubs and trees. In the distance were dark hills covered with scattered vegetation. The scene was bleak, yet in a strange way rather beautiful.

We used the largest pieces of mast and spar for upright beams, which we sank in the ground to form a rectangular frame about fifteen feet wide and six feet deep. Not having nails or hammer, we had to tie the crossbeams with salvaged lines and cords. We lashed small boards together and placed them on the frame at an angle to make the sides and the top. The top we covered with pieces of sails we had found on the beach. Some were long enough to extend down over the sides. Our opening was on the east side, and we covered the floor with a sort of dry grass that had a downy, cotton-like flower. With the cotton cloth, needle, and thread we had salvaged from the wreckage Captain Costa made a large sheet to cover us at night.

By now I suppose I should have felt our situation was much

‡ Modern topographic maps show a two-hundred-foot-high hill near this location. It is aptly named Camp Hill.

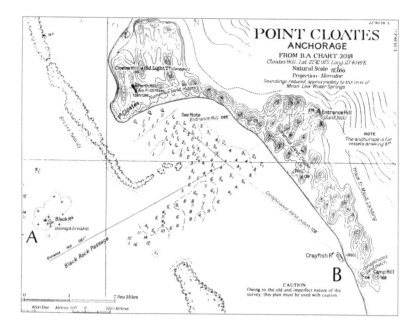

improved, but my mind was elsewhere even while I helped build the camp. I wondered what the country was like. We knew almost nothing at all about it, just as we knew nothing about the African countries we had passed months ago. Perhaps my cousin Miloslavich would have known; he had been well educated—but he was dead. All I knew was that the English had sent many convicts to this land and that other free settlers had come to establish a British colony. But I didn't know where they were—whether they were along this coast or perhaps inland a bit. I thought we should talk about it, and soon. I tried to forget stories I had heard about cannibals.

I seemed to be the only one worrying about these things. No one wanted to talk about the things that were bothering me, but everyone was concerned about food. We needed to eat to regain our strength. Taking care of that need was to be our task the second day ashore. We had food, but no fire, and we really needed warm food. I remembered the sextant case among the objects washed ashore and hurried to find it among our stores. Costa had already cleaned it earlier in the day and used it to take a sun sighting to establish the position of the shipwreck. He had to estimate because he didn't know the time of day that would give

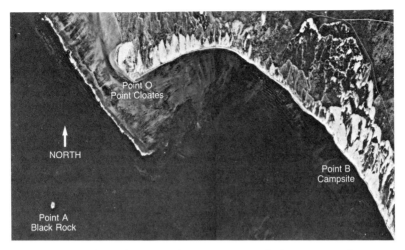

Hydrographic chart (scale 1:75,000) of the Point Cloates area (opposite page) and a satellite photograph (scale 1:40,000) of Black Rock (Point A)—white breaking waves; Point Cloates (Point O), the campsite (Point B)

him an exact fix. He determined that the approximate location of the shipwreck was nine miles west-northwest from where we stood, or about 22°48' meridian latitude, and 113°37'40" longitude.*

But my interest in the sextant was its lenses. I carefully removed one and used it to focus the sun's rays on some dry leaves and twigs. All I got was smoke, but someone suggested adding a little of the gunpowder we had found in the chest. In a second, there was a loud explosion as the powder ignited and shattered the lens and burned my arm. My pride in my accomplishment was also shattered. Someone used some of the olive oil and salvaged linen to bandage my arm. I was to carry the scar for life. Nevertheless,

---

* A remarkably accurate estimate considering the circumstances and unknowns. Modern charts show Black Rock as the closest underwater obstruction—about two miles north and slightly east of the latitude and longitude given. The other evidence that suggests that Black Rock was the point of impact includes the facts that there are no other rocks within a two-mile radius, the reefs are only three miles offshore, rather than nine, and there is a wide, clear passage through the reefs from Black Rock to shore. (See chart on opposite page.) In their recent diving operations in the vicinity, the maritime archaeologists of the Western Australian Museum have examined Black Rock but found no evidence of the wreck other than a trail of coal on the seabed closer to the beach.[1]

a fine blaze was soon burning, with some of the *Stefano*'s wreckage as fuel.

Someone made a thick paste of flour and a tiny bit of our precious water, kneaded it into a dough, and baked it in a tar-stained can we had found. The warm bread was delicious in spite of the tar flavor imparted by the baking pan and the sand which had somehow gotten into the dough. We also warmed a can of meat to round out our first hot meal since the shipwreck. No one talked while we ate. I tried to block out thoughts of those who had died and also of those back home whom I might never see again. I wanted to sleep to escape the thoughts that I did not want to think. But sleep didn't come easily to me that night. I wept most of the night and arose weak and quite despondent.

Fortunately, there were plenty of things to keep our minds and spirits occupied during the day. We had to keep a constant watch on the fire. We made a daily search along the shore, and inland, for food—mostly small fish and crustaceans. And there was the daily trip from the camp to the water cask, about two miles north.

This routine continued uneventfully for several days. By now I was even more anxious to know exactly where we were and how we could have run aground if we had been fifteen to twenty miles offshore heading northwest some six to eight hours before we struck. I could have asked Costa while we were alone tending the fire, but I didn't because I didn't want him to feel that I blamed him in some way.

Suddenly my thoughts were interrupted by a sight that nearly stopped my heart. A large group of black savages was descending a small hill next to our camp and heading directly toward us. Men, women, and children were all naked and some carried crude weapons. I was terrified. I had heard horror stories about the wild men of these tropical seas—tales of atrocities and cannibalism. Even though I hadn't believed the stories, I wanted to hide. But we were in the open; there was no bush or brush large enough to conceal me. I was ready to run even though I knew their walking speed was faster than any sprint I could maintain. Several of the crew who were fishing nearby saw the frightening sight and, to my relief, rushed toward us.

Jurich, with amazing composure, shouted, "The water—the cask of water! Run with me quickly to guard it!" Several of the crew dashed north along the beach to the precious water keg while the others came up to the camp.

By the time Jurich reached the water, the natives were rolling and tossing the cask about as if it were a huge toy. This wasn't at all funny to Jurich and the others. Because the innocents' game could cost us our only water supply, Jurich, with commendable courage, walked boldly up to the blacks and by signs more than words tried to make them understand our situation. With a sense almost of reverence, they abandoned their game and directed all of their attention on us. They conducted a thorough, but gentle, examination of us intruders. Our limbs, hair, and scanty articles of clothing were inspected. We were frightened, especially because of the dangerous-looking spears they carried in their right hands and the strange short, curved sticks they held in the left.

Suddenly they seemed to lose interest in us, and as quickly as they had come, they left our camp and went to the shore. We breathed sighs of relief. I came out from the farthest corner of the shelter where I had been trying to hide and saw Captain Costa following the natives.

The natives were searching for small crabs and clams and were finding them rather easily. Whenever they found something, they never failed to offer it to Costa before partaking themselves. Encouraged by this kindness and their earlier gentleness, Costa spoke to them in English and French alternately, asking them the location of Champion Bay (south of Shark Bay), which he felt must be within range. The natives merely repeated his words as best they could, occasionally adding a few words in their own language. It was frustrating because we now felt they wanted to help us but wouldn't be able to if we couldn't make them understand our need to know our whereabouts. They seemed puzzled and they seemed to want to help. While they were talking among themselves, one man approached Costa, as if in awe of him, and handed him a piece of paper which he had found on the rocks near the shore.

It was more than unbelievable, it was miraculous. The paper he found was a piece from one of the *Stefano*'s charts of the northwest coast of Australia. The salvaged piece showed not only the area we were in but also the destination Costa had in mind —the Gascoyne River. Looking at the chart, Costa was able to pinpoint where we had come ashore—about 22°48′ latitude, just south of what, on our chart, was called Klute's Point.*

The Gascoyne River was 2° south (24°50′). Costa thought that was the most likely spot to find a small white settlement. And, best of all, it was—or he thought it was—within walking distance even given our present condition. Costa was optimistic. He happily said it was "only eighty miles away, which we should be able to cover in eight to ten days. We start tomorrow!"† We were overjoyed at the prospect of reaching a settlement. The natives seemed to fail to understand our joy but also seemed indifferent to any possible reason for us to be joyful. They graciously shared with us some meager red and black beans they had gathered. They ate them raw and drank large quantities of water after eating. The meal made them joyful. When we crawled under our small piece of sail about midnight, the savages quietly left us and went due north up the coast.

The next morning was completely calm and clear for the first time since we had washed ashore. It was November 1, All Saints' Day. Shortly after sunrise, we carefully hid or buried whatever goods and provisions we could not readily carry. We took with us twelve bottles of wine and twelve of water, a few cans of salted meat, a keg of flour, and some beans. We were counting on finding some source of fresh water along the way. And we knew we would have to count on shellfish, crabs, and whatever else the seashore might yield when our small food supply was exhausted. Costa would not leave until he finished carving the names of the ship and her crew, living and dead, on a cabin door from the *Stefano*. The door was now a part of the shelter we had built.

A large piece of linen we had salvaged from the wreck was torn into strips to wrap our tender feet, which were quite sore from insect bites and small cuts made by the tough grass, thorns, and rocks. The precious fire which I had started was extinguished; I

* Point Cloates on the Royal Navy charts of the period—King, 1818–22; Flinders, 1803.

† This was a very critical decision for Costa. He knew food and water would not last long at the campsite, so he realized they would have to walk their way out. He was accurate about the Gascoyne River being 2° south. But he certainly must have known that 1° equals 60 nautical miles, so the total distance to be walked was not 80 miles but 120 miles. Baccich could not have misunderstood, considering the reference to an eight- to ten-day walk.

felt a sense of loss as it vanished. We went quickly lest we be tempted to remain. We left the shoreline and traveled inland so we could set a straight course rather than follow the much longer line of the beach. Besides, a nice grassy plain, the inland route, promised relief from the discomfort of the burning sand. Once again, we proved to be naïve. What seemed to be an inviting field of cool grass was a mat of tough leaves, thorns, and thistles that lacerated our legs and feet. It even shredded our clothing. By midday the sun forced us to carry a large sheet of sailcloth above our heads. It didn't really help. This far inland, there were no cool breezes from the Indian Ocean to provide even occasional relief from the scorching heat.

By the middle of the second afternoon, we were almost completely exhausted. It made matters worse to realize that we couldn't walk twenty miles in two days even when we were not suffering from thirst or starvation. We wondered if we would be able to do anything at all in a few days. We had found no water at all and, after the first day, no food except the unpalatable shellfish, and even these appeared to be getting scarcer.

To everyone's surprise, the first one to give way under the mental and physical strain was Costa. Toward the end of the third day's march [Point C, near Point Maud], he threw himself on the ground and insisted he was unable to take another step. He urged and then commanded us to leave him behind to die so that we might have a better chance to save ourselves. Then, as if he knew I was destined to survive, he addressed me. "When you are saved and see our homeland again, remember my charge to you. Carry my final greeting to my dear mother and to my sister Amelia. Tell them I died with their names in my heart and on my lips."

Several of us wept aloud. Although I was the youngest and least experienced, I was sure I knew why Costa had collapsed this way. It was certainly not just physical. He seemed to hold himself responsible for our situation and to feel we would not survive. Guilt and self-blame had overcome him.

I must confess that as the shock of the shipwreck wore off, I certainly speculated about who was to blame. I wondered how such a mistake could occur unless there had been negligence on someone's part. I knew who was at the helm holding a northeast course when the situation plainly called for northwest, but I haven't recorded his name. I don't know if Costa or Miloslavich gave a wrong order to the helmsman. But it seemed as if Costa faulted himself because at sea the senior man is always responsible for the safety of his ship and his men, regardless of circumstances.

I wasn't willing to let Costa punish himself. Not only was I a friend, I was a blood relative. Without hesitating, I tried to pick him up to carry him. I found myself saying, "Dear Costa, we became a burden to you when Miloslavich died. I won't be a burden to you any longer. It is time for us to carry you, who have carried us so well for the past seven days." The other men quickly helped support Costa. To this day, I wonder where my words came from and how I was able to speak so forcefully.

After two or three more days, we were near Cape Anderson. On November 7, we crossed the Tropic of Capricorn, with Costa once more our leader. He never again uttered a word of distress, but we had barely recovered from that crisis when another occurred. In midafternoon on the seventh, Jurich, Bucich, and Vulovich—overcome by fatigue, thirst, and heat—collapsed on the burning sand [Point D]. This latest misfortune posed a real dilemma for us. We didn't know whether to abandon our shipmates and push on in hopes of saving ourselves and perhaps the ones we were leaving behind as well, or to stay with them with less hope that any of us would survive. We decided to leave the three, at least temporarily, to see if some haven of comfort and safety or even water or food could be found ahead.

We walked all of the next day and part of the night, always on hard rocks or thorny brush, but we found no water or food. We didn't know that only a few yards inland was a well-known footpath used by the savages. Unfortunately, the possibility that such a path existed never occurred to us.

When we stopped in the middle of the night to rest, I tried to estimate how far we had come from our original camp and how far we had yet to go to reach the Gascoyne River and its expected settlement. We had started on the afternoon of November 1 and it was now the eighth. Some time was lost during daylight hours because of the heat and the exhaustion it caused, but we usually made up for this by walking part of the night. We had walked a total of eight days. I don't think we fell short of the plan we had to average ten miles a day. Costa had told us our goal was only eight to ten days away. Surely tomorrow or the next day we should reach it. Yet it was only yesterday morning that we were sure we had come upon Cape Anderson—or at least what seemed to be Cape Anderson according to the precious fragment of map which Costa carried.

I began to tremble when I realized that Costa's original estimate could not be correct! Only two degrees south, he had said—only eighty miles, eight to ten days. What had he got us into?

After I calmed down, I recalculated our position and soon knew the horrible truth. Last night, only fifteen miles back, we had crossed the Tropic of Capricorn, slightly north of Cape Farquhar. At that point we would have been 1°30' north of the Gascoyne River because the Tropic of Capricorn is at 23°30' south. We had covered only one quarter of the distance we thought we would have to cover to reach our goal. That meant instead of being one or two days from our goal, we were not even halfway. We had at least six to eight more days to travel. It was as if we were just starting out; only now we were weakened by thirst and hunger.

I didn't know if I should confront Costa with my disturbing conclusion. I didn't know what effect such knowledge would have on my shipmates, and I could be wrong. Perhaps Costa had deliberately misled us because he understood our need to feel encouraged. I finally fell asleep without having answered any of the questions I had put to myself.

The next day everyone was in reasonably good spirits. Costa and I must have been the only two who knew we could not reach our destination by sundown or even the next day. Before starting out, Dediol had the good sense to bury the keg of flour he was carrying because he could no longer bear even the small amount of extra exertion it took to carry it. The day's walk was very short. No more than half the day had passed when fatigue and thirst brought us to a standstill. However, luck was with us—we came upon the first natural shelter in all of the bleak area we had covered after being cast ashore. We saw a rocky ridge that came down to within a few yards of the shoreline. The side facing the beach had eroded and formed a shallow cave about twenty feet wide and ten to twenty feet high. It provided the first shade we had found. Not only did it protect us from the sun, it also gave us some protection from the strong wind and, we were to discover that night, it gave us some warmth. The rocks, heated by the sun, slowly released that heat throughout the chilly night. With Costa's map, we were able to determine that we were at the north edge of Cape Farquhar. Although we didn't know it yet, we were destined to spend many days and suffer much at this location [Point E].

We couldn't really appreciate the relief this pleasant location might provide us because our hunger and our thirst were so great. We had only one small bottle of water and about a pound of flour for six men.

Suddenly a rustling in the brush beside the cave caught our attention, and a moment later two stalwart savages appeared in our midst. Under any other circumstances, the sight of these ferocious and frightfully armed creatures might have filled us with fear and panic. But our earlier experience with the natives hadn't given us cause for concern, and what could be worse than the plight we were already in? None of us was afraid that these wild men would torture us. Our only reaction was to follow them with our eyes. They seemed just as curious about us as the first group we had met. The one nearest me came over and started to feel my arms and touch my skin, which was still quite pale and soft compared to his. My tattered shreds of clothing were, for the second time, subjected to a detailed examination.

The native's facial expression and gestures suggested that he understood we were dying of thirst and hunger. The Aborigines tried to talk to us, but their phrases were unintelligible. It was far easier to guess their meaning from their gestures. They wanted us to follow them. I didn't see why we shouldn't, so I led our group from the shelter. On this, our second meeting with the savages, there was again only gentleness and curiosity and not the brutality we previously attributed to them. They rapidly led us from the shore until we reached a narrow, well-worn path leading east toward a gently sloping hill. Beyond the hill was a grassy plain, delightful and inviting. There were many flowering plants and shrubs—a vision of paradise for our eyes, which were tired of the monotonous glare and heat from the burning sands. The natives searched the plain as if looking for something left behind. Suddenly they seemed to find what they were looking for. It was a shallow indentation in the ground—about a foot deep and partially covered over with tree bark and dried brush. They peered intently at this hole in the ground. We gathered around, but we couldn't see anything at all. The savages suddenly began digging in the sandy soil with their bare hands, and soon the sand they were removing appeared damp. As fast as they withdrew the damp earth, they deposited it along the walls of the growing hole to form a stronger surface and to prevent drier soil from tumbling back into the excavation.

We were wild with delight at the sight of the damp sand. Half-frantic with thirst, we greedily grabbed handfuls of wet dirt and stuffed it in our mouths. The natives, evidently unconcerned about our strange behavior, continued digging and walling to a depth of about five feet, where clear fresh water streamed into the hole. The natives seemed puzzled by our exuberance and joy. We hurriedly gulped cooling drafts—once, twice, three times.

We filled the empty bottles that we had carried for the past ten days in anticipation of finding water. Like the well, my heart suddenly overflowed with gratitude to our black Moses who had miraculously wrung water from the rocks of the desert to save us from perishing.

As if in return for services rendered, the two savages, by words and gestures, insisted on having the small jar of flour which we had been hoarding. Considering the water they had just obtained for us, we couldn't refuse, and willingly handed over our little treasure. In just a few seconds, one of the pair had started a fire with a bunch of dried twigs they had gathered. He did it so quickly that none of us knew how he could have done it. The other savage produced a hollowed stone on which he mixed a paste of the flour and water and set it, stone included, on the hot fire to bake. In about fifteen minutes, the baked bread was taken from the fire, and, wonders never ceasing, the two blacks, instead of eating the bread themselves, presented the whole loaf to Costa.

Their generosity brought tears to my eyes and Costa blinked and shyly wiped his cheeks. Although we had not had any food since the previous day, Costa without hesitation divided the small loaf and returned the first share to our benefactors, and what a feast we had—bread and water.

As soon as the meal was finished, the savages made it clear by signs that they would leave us and continue north. Costa, now quite reassured about the natives, decided I should go with them to locate and recover the keg of flour that Dediol had buried early the day before because of his fatigue. Even though it was only several miles away and should take only an hour or so, I wasn't at all happy about going and tried to pass the chore on to Dediol, who would certainly remember exactly where he hid the treasure. But Dediol had already generously volunteered for what appeared to be a tougher and more important task—to carry some water from our new source back to where we had left our three shipmates two days before. Two others were going with him; Costa was to scour the beach for something we could eat, and Lovrinovich would guard the fire and keep it going.

There wasn't any way for me to avoid going even though I was seriously afraid of these two savages. They understood that I was supposed to go with them and were trying to get me to precede them on the track. Although I knew they were helping us, I was still trembling and on the verge of panic as I hurried along the track ahead of them. Two brief encounters with Aborigines, although enlightening, were not enough to replace the warnings that I had heard and read during my life: "Beware of the black barbarians—the cannibals!"

By this time the two natives were impatient with my slow pace on the track and passed me by. They moved ahead about fifty feet and kept looking back and signaling me to walk faster. Even when they walked at their slowest speed, I couldn't keep up. I thought to myself how magnificent they looked, almost floating through the tangled brush. They moved so effortlessly!

After watching them awhile, I began to realize I was more like them than I was different from them. Except for color, we have the same physical characteristics, and after days under the tropical sun, I could see that I, too, would be black or nearly black if I had spent my life naked in this climate. By this time my fears had almost completely subsided and I found myself, in some strange way, envious of these men. How could my shipmates and I be so utterly helpless in this land when these primitive men were so completely capable? If they could find all of life's necessities in the wilderness, why couldn't we? I knew one way or another I could prove equal to them. I could learn. I knew I was superior to them in so many ways—ways they could never learn. But most important, by baptism I had become one of the children of God, an heir to life everlasting. These savages, on the other hand, could never enter the kingdom of heaven. I reminded myself that we owed our lives to them. Maybe I could baptize them; I wished that they were white.

By now the natives were chanting, "Bulava, bulava." I came

to understand that this was their simple imitation of the English word "flour, flour." They obviously knew what I was being sent to find. A little later, I realized I couldn't hear or see them. I became frightened and turned to run full speed back to where I had left Costa. Before I got to the top of the first hill, three fierce-looking and heavily armed savages appeared out of nowhere. I froze. They didn't pay any attention to me but quietly continued on their way. They left the track and vanished into the bush. This experience convinced me to turn around and rejoin the two natives I had started with in order to retrieve the flour as Costa had ordered me to do. Unfortunately, I arrived too late. The keg had been unearthed and emptied, so I had to return empty-handed. I rejoined Costa about nightfall. We shared a few clams, then dug the usual holes in the sand for our tired bodies. I soon found deep, restful sleep.

Meanwhile Jurich, Bucich, and Vulovich, the three we left behind two days before (about fifteen miles north), rested only half a day and then rose in the middle of the night to try to rejoin us. They walked all night and into the following day, until the tropical heat once again overcame them. This time they prayed for a speedy death rather than rescue—anything to stop their misery. But rescue of a sort it was to be, probably by members of the same tribe from which our two visitors came. A large band of natives, numbering about fifty, came upon our shipmates, who were prostrate and near death. Without hesitation the natives carried them to a nearby well. The fresh water provided an almost miraculous cure for our shipmates. With revived spirits and renewed energy, they were able to walk with the tribe to a nearby clearing, where the natives started a fire and cooked a bountiful meal of baked fish. The three famished castaways could not cease wondering at the great generosity of these wild ones.

Hope as well as energy had been restored and they knew their chances of catching up with us had improved, especially after Jurich discovered what he was sure were our footprints in the sand nearby. These tracks evidently made the same impression on the savages because two of them immediately began following the trail, motioning the three whites to follow them. Leaving the small plain, they moved inland somewhat and went south about a mile until they came to a remarkable oasis. Fresh flowering shrubs were abundant and there was soft grassy ground cover in a large open area that was surrounded by trees. This must have been a frequent rendezvous point for native tribes; there were mounds of litter scattered around. There was a small hill resembling a volcanic crater in the middle of the plain. On the east side of the hill there was a small clear, cool pond [Point F]. We later learned that this place to which our shipmates were taken was only about three miles north of the spot where the rest of us had found relief [Point E].

Jurich and his companions had barely noticed the beauty of the spot when the rest of the tribe arrived from the north and were joined almost immediately by another tribe from the south or east. This meeting seemed prearranged. The tribes quickly intermingled and people greeted each other excitedly. There were now about 130 men, women, and children—many strangely armed. I didn't know until I heard this account that I hadn't been alone in fearing the blacks. The three men were huddled together in a feeble attempt to gain strength and comfort when a startled cry arose from within the crowd of newly arrived savages—"Brothers! Brothers!" the voice shrieked excitedly. In another moment the one who had cried out emerged from the throng, still calling out in our mother tongue.

It was Perancich, who, up to that moment, had been counted among the dead who had gone down with the *Stefano*. The meeting with one presumed dead was extremely affecting. When the details were repeated to me later, I found myself moved to tears.

Perancich told how a heavy wave swept over the ship as he was trying to loose one of the *Stefano*'s lifeboats from its moorings. He was washed overboard from the spars to join, or so we thought at the time, young Harry Groiss as the first of the fatalities. However, Perancich surfaced in the lee of the sinking ship amid thick wreckage—timber, sails, and lines of the crumbling ship— and he clung to the mess with the strength of despair. His battle against death lasted throughout the night and all of the following day. Toward evening he was washed ashore, more dead than alive, at a point we calculated to be ten miles south of where the rest of us had landed. It was the only place for many miles where a break in the chain of offshore reefs allowed one to reach the beach safely. Perancich took shelter under an overhanging rock formation near the shore and spent two days eating sweet, watery berries that grew near the shore in order to gain some strength.

The third day, while searching for water and other food, he met the band of savages. Instead of harming him, they provided for him, sharing whatever food and drink they found in the wilderness—yet another example of the unexpected generosity of the wild men we had been taught about in school.

Following Perancich's narrative of his experience, Jurich recounted our own adventures to date and then suggested that all four of them should head toward the shore, where they would have the best chance of joining the rest of us. When they reached the beach, they saw Brajevich, Antoncich, and Dediol heading toward them, carrying the supply of water. Antoncich was especially happy to see Perancich because they were lifelong friends from the island of Mali Lošinj in the Kvarner Gulf.

The seven men headed south and, after walking about three miles, joined Costa, Lovrinovich, and me at the well [Point E], where we were tending our fire and gathering food. After this third reunion, we had a little food and water and dug in for a well-earned rest. It had been a day filled with much emotion.

For the first time since the wreck, our party numbered ten. It was November 8, only twelve days after we struck Black Rock, but it seemed an eternity.‡ According to our fragment of a map, we were at or near Cape Farquhar. We had walked only sixty or seventy miles in eight days. By my reckoning, we still had about fifty miles to go to reach the Gascoyne River and civilization.

The following day we felt unable to start our march, so we lay about and enjoyed our abundant supply of water and scant supply of berries and shellfish. I was quite restless all day. I was anxious to move on because I knew we had at least five or six days' journey ahead, and I knew we would tire quickly because of our condition. The journey could take twice as long as my estimate. In any event, the sooner we started, the better our chances for success. Early on the morning of the tenth we started, and after the first day's march, I knew we were in for trouble and disappointment. The effects of continued deprivation quickly drained our reserves

‡ The date of November 8 was also given by Baccich on page 24. This suggests the unlikelihood that the survivors could keep an exact tally of days and dates in spite of their subsequent claim to the contrary. Rather than change the specific dates cited or alter the descriptions of the intervening daily events, the inconsistencies have been left throughout. The cumulative error over several months, however, was insignificant, plus or minus one or two days.

of energy. We were barely able to cover five miles in a day, half of what we had averaged at first.

After five days, we had just passed the 24th parallel and we were down to two days' supply of water. We were no longer able to find berries and edible plants without going so far inland as to lose sight of the ocean, our only reference point. We had covered thirty miles and had at least that many to go. Shortly before sundown, we saw in the distance a refreshing-looking stream winding across the land down to the ocean. It was partly concealed by the sand dunes and the brush. Surely this must be the river that would lead us to a settlement—to civilization and rescue. This prospect gave us new strength and enabled us to push on for a few more hours until we reached what seemed to be the head of the stream [Point G]. Lying scattered around were large piles of seashells and skeletons of what we thought must have been wild dogs. But, unfortunately, there was no sign of a stream. Apparently, what we had seen was nothing more than a narrow coastal inlet which interrupted an otherwise straight shoreline. Our buoyant hopes disappeared quickly and we waded through the salty, sticky marsh to reach its southern side in order to save the few extra steps and effort that would have been needed to walk around this small inlet—about a half mile in length and only a hundred feet across.

How we managed to push on the next day—November 16—I do not know. But we did, and in the afternoon we passed Cape Cuvier. We were half-starved, down to our last bottle of water, fully baked by the sun—sore, bruised, and bleeding—and filled with despair. I had the will and strength to go on because I knew the Gascoyne River couldn't be more than twenty to twenty-five miles away—two days at best, three at most.

But only Costa and Bucich shared my feelings. In fact, a mutiny began to develop the evening of the sixteenth when seven members of our group declared they would no longer go south. They felt uncertain about the distance ahead because we had already walked farther than originally planned. More important, their thirst and suffering made them crave the pleasant surroundings of the wells and shelter back at Cape Farquhar [Points E and F].

Costa told them they were free to head back without any comment from him concerning the propriety of their action, but he felt a duty to continue south to lead us to the place he believed offered the best possibility for rescue. After an exchange of good wishes that, for the most part, hid the pain of our sorrowful parting from our friends, Costa, Bucich, and I started out. We had barely got out of sight of our shipmates when Costa exclaimed, "I cannot abandon them! We must stay together, to live or die as one." And in an instant we had turned around and hastened to rejoin our friends [Point H].

I confess my mixed feelings about this development. On the one hand, I had enormous respect and affection for Costa and would never call into question, much less challenge, his decision. But I was disappointed we had quit when we were so close to our goal.* Even worse, we now had no plan for rescue, or even survival, and it seemed that our concerns were only for the moment—water, food, shelter for one day at a time. We seemed to have given up trying to save ourselves. Luckily, we discovered a smooth, straight inland path which not only shortened the return distance considerably but was much easier on our feet than the shoreline would have been. We were equally fortunate in finding juicy, nourishing berries along our route.

---

* Had the group continued on to the Gascoyne, which, as Baccich surmised, was only some twenty miles away, it would not have meant immediate salvation, for there was no permanent settlement at the river's mouth in 1875. Indeed, at that time of year they would have been lucky if they had found as much as a pool or two lying in the otherwise dry bed of a large ravine. However, eventually they might have been able to make contact with a vessel plying the northern approaches to the vast Shark Bay, a scene of pearling operations.

4

Cave of Death

We arrived back at the cape [Cape Farquhar: Point E] about five or six days later (November 21 or 22) and established ourselves in the large cool cave near the seashore where Costa and I had stayed the night when, with four others, we first discovered it two weeks earlier.

I was happy and felt rested during the ten days we spent at this unusual spot. However, my mind kept straying to such worrisome things as the improbability of rescue at this location. I felt the very least we could do was to collect enough wood and brush for a signal fire in case we eventually sighted a ship in this area. Before I could suggest this, we had to abandon our garden-like spot because we had completely exhausted the small supply of mollusks and crabs on the shore, as well as the berries and seeds we found inland. So we decided to move north about three miles to the little oasis [Point F] where we had first discovered the missing Perancich.

The food supply was indeed better. We discovered a very plentiful bean, which grew on a slender climbing vine and was yellowish, somewhat similar to the European red bean.* But we needed a fire to prepare it properly. Every attempt we made failed, even though we carefully imitated the savages and used the same materials that worked so well for them.

* Possibly the Canavalia, or jack bean.

Camp Farquhar area. This satellite photograph covers the area three miles southwest of Cape Farquhar to six miles northwest of the cape. It includes Points E and F from the 1876 map. The area today is much like it was over a hundred years ago—no roads or tracks—and is probably still the wildest, remotest stretch along the western coast of the continent

We had carefully preserved a few grains of gunpowder to help start a fire, but first we had to produce a spark. We still had the steel blade from one of the carpenter's planes that had been salvaged the day after the shipwreck. This gave Perancich the idea of flint and steel—a widely used sparking device. But we didn't know where we would find a flint. Eventually, someone found a small flint-like stone, and Perancich, for the most part unnoticed by the rest of us, began nonchalantly rubbing stone and steel together with little hope of success. Suddenly there was a flash and a faint explosion. A spark had touched the gunpowder and a small blaze flickered brightly. We were joyful and some hurried off for more twigs and firewood. Others went to gather beans and get water.

When our first hot meal in about a month was ready, Perancich, to the astonishment of the rest of us, reached out to grab all that we had cooked. "Poor fellow," I thought, "he is usually so calm and quiet. We must sympathize with his starved condition." A few hours after eating, we all had severe stomach pains, but at the time no one seemed to connect the sickness with the beans. Had we only known earlier what we would later learn from the savages! The beans should be eaten only in very small quantities because of the concentrated richness and only after being baked in the hot sand for a few days, soaked in water for two more days, and then boiled. There was much we civilized men did not understand.

Fishing was a daily necessity and the task fell to me. I actually enjoyed it and looked forward to my short walk from the well to the shore, where I spent most of the day. One day I discovered quite a large fish trapped where the high tide had left it in a pool above the shoreline. In my eagerness to capture it, I carelessly thrust my hands into the water and grabbed at it. In an instant the fish closed its jaws on my hand and made an ugly, deep wound. It was with great difficulty that I was able to free my hand. The wound was painful and was to heal very slowly. I was to carry a lifelong scar. For the next week or so, I had to care for my hand carefully and regularly. Because I could not fish or tolerate any exertion, I journeyed south back to the cool shade of our first shelter [Point E]. Vulovich joined me at the cave the next day. He had cut his foot on sharp rocks while gathering shellfish. When I recuperated enough to rejoin the group, I left Vulovich at the cave.

The worst misfortune of those early days spent at the two waterholes was the obvious decline of Perancich. Beginning with the day when he tried to grab all of the food, he acted like one in a trance. He seemed to have no thought or feeling for his companions, hid by himself in the bush most of the time, and was constantly smiling. He dashed about nervously, sometimes walked backwards, and never uttered a word. We allowed him to do as he pleased and never said anything about his strangeness, not to him, nor among ourselves. But it was obvious to us, in spite of our silence, that he had gone mad.

To compound our problems, the weather turned bad. It was the hurricane, or cyclone, season for that latitude, and we soon experienced the full brunt of a tropical storm. Unlike hurricanes in the northern hemisphere, which circulate counterclockwise, moving north from the equator, and eventually drifting to the east, these cyclones moved south from the equator, generally in a westerly drift, and were preceded by strong hot, dry winds. On December 21 we had the prelude to such a storm. Although there was no rain, the tide was much higher than usual and heavy surf was breaking fiercely over the offshore reef and swelling along the usually calm shoreline. The creatures of the sea must have known what was about to happen. They had all disappeared— gone to deeper water, I guessed. We found no fish, crabs, or clams that day. By afternoon, the wind had risen beyond gale force, and even though there was still no rain, there were low-hanging clouds everywhere.

I don't know why we waited so long to prepare ourselves for the storm. When the rains came at day's end, the effect was terrifying. We were blinded by the wind-driven water, which stung us painfully. It was bone-chilling, and too late we knew that we needed better shelter if we were to survive the night. In unison we shouted to one another, "To the old cave!" We were not at all sure we could make it, though it was only three miles away.

We were so accustomed to not having enough water that it seemed strange to be tortured now by so much. Perhaps that explains our negligence. By the time we were in the downpour, the wind prevented us from standing upright. We crawled, or dragged ourselves, across the soggy land. Large clumps of brush, sticks, and other debris were being blown about as we moved in a southerly direction, and we had to shield ourselves from the punishing blows of the wind-driven mess as best we could.

Every few minutes, flashes of lightning blinded me. When my eyes readjusted, I could see that our group had been dispersed. Some had settled for what little shelter a small clump of bushes or rocks provided. Others continued to press ahead. Our shouts to one another seemed mere whispers in the raging storm.

At about midnight, Jurich and Dediol reached the cave. Their relief was short-lived; hours went by and no one joined them. Moreover, Vulovich, who was expected to be recuperating in the cave, was not there. There was no real rest for them, and at dawn they ventured out of the cave because the storm appeared to have blown over. The rain had stopped and directly overhead the sky was clear. Trees, brush, logs, even sizable boulders and clumps of coral were strewn everywhere. Seaweed uprooted from the ocean floor was piled high along the shore—and there was not a sign of another living creature anywhere. The wind had stripped the leaves from every bush and tree in sight. The naked limbs were coated with salt spray, which began to glisten as the sun started to dry them out. The sky clouded up again after the two men had made a short, futile search along the shore.[†] After the second storm, they saw two pitiful creatures struggling toward them as they emerged from the cave. Costa and I had survived. By nightfall, one or two arriving at a time, there were eight of us together at the cave. Perancich and Vulovich, one mad and the other lame, were still missing.

This was probably the worst day in my life. I was cold, wet, hungry, and thirsty; my wounded hand ached all the way to my shoulder. Two friends were missing. I was filled with despair.

Overcome by all this misery, I sought a remote corner of the cave in hopes that my muffled sobs would bring me some measure of the comfort I needed. In such a state of deprivation, it is strange how little is needed to bring relief. First a spark, then a little flame, lit up the cave. Antoncich had carried the flint and iron safely through the storm with him and had miraculously coaxed a fire in the midst of all this wetness. How good the shadowy faces of my friends looked after the darkness! One, most familiar, moved closer. Costa bent over, grasped my shoulder, and smiled down at me. "Merry Christmas, Miho," he said.[‡]

The following day, Jurich, Dediol, and I left the cave early to search for Perancich and Vulovich. It was a bright, beautiful morning—clear, dry, and cool. We knew we had only a short

---

[†] This description suggests that the eye of the cyclone must have been passing right over the area of the cave. After the eye passes, the force of the hurricane returns but with less strength than that felt preceding the center. The diameter of the eye measures a mile or more across. This phenomenon can be seen today in weather satellite photographs of tropical storms, when there is sometimes a clear sky, with no rain for several hours and a much lower wind velocity.

[‡] On January 14, 1876, the *West Australian Times* reported that at least four ships and fifty-nine lives were lost in the Exmouth Gulf area, when a violent cyclone struck that locality on December 24 and 25 before moving south.

time to search because everyone had agreed to move inland to hunt for food. The storm had devastated every growing thing along the shore, and we didn't know when we would be able to get food from the sea. We hadn't gone a hundred yards from the cave when we saw the sad sight we feared. Although not unexpected, it was still heartbreaking. Poor Perancich, without a sound mind to guide his footsteps, had dropped in his tracks only minutes from help. He had died alone. His poor water-ravaged frame, half on the sand, half on the grass, lay like flotsam with the logs that surrounded him. We didn't speak but silently signaled to beckon the others, who were emerging from the cave, to join us. We stood around his body silent and motionless for some time until Antoncich, his childhood friend and neighbor, broke the spell by beginning to dig a grave beside the place Perancich had fallen. With our help the sad task was finished, and we laid him tenderly to rest, chanting as much of the Divine Office for the Dead as we could remember.

Only a few days later the corpse of Vulovich was discovered— no farther from the cave than Perancich's body had been. We would have seen it sooner, but he had fallen into a crevice. By now the corpse was in an advanced state of decomposition, and it was actually the odor that enabled us to find him. Again we dug a grave with our hands and, for the third time, laid a brother in his final resting place.

Over the next thirty days I saw six more of my comrades perish in this same area [Points E and F, near Cape Farquhar]. We did almost nothing but wait for death with no thought of rescue. Our only activity was to search harder and longer for ever-scarcer food.

The one thing we tried to do to improve our lot failed. A few days after the storm, about December 28, Lovrinovich decided he should try to walk back to our original campsite because we had buried a supply of food there. No one but Brajevich was interested in accompanying him. The distance was great—about seventy or eighty miles, seven to ten days' walk each way at least. The two left with as much bottled water as they could carry and a small amount of wild beans and a little of our last bit of flour. They were back in three days, having given up the trip because of hunger and weakness. We were now certain that all we could do was wait patiently for a miraculous, unanticipated rescue or for death.

In the week that followed, all of us did less and less. Two or three didn't move about at all. The range of our travel was now limited to the distance between the waterhole near the shore [Point F] and our cave and well [Point E]—three miles. Fortunately, we had discovered another cave near the waterhole, very close to where the path met the ocean. It was barely sixty yards from the sea, in the side of a cliff right below the elevated plain, and was about sixteen square feet. Now we had good shelter at both spots.

Costa, my closest friend, was the next to leave us. Because he was like a brother to me, sometimes even like a father, it is upsetting to describe his last days. But I must note how much we all loved and respected him. He hadn't sought the authority he had over us, but neither did he shirk the responsibility when it was thrust upon him. He accepted it and discharged his duties with honor and sacrifice. At the age of twenty-four he had acted like a patriarch of three times his age and wisdom, and the reverence we felt toward him was evident when we discussed what must be done if we were to save him.

Although seeing our leader so stricken further demoralized our little band, Lovrinovich, who had recently failed in the attempt to return to our original campsite, once again volunteered to make the trip and recover food and wine hidden there. This time he would go for Costa, and he swore he would not fail again. Brajevich, his companion on the first attempt, once more pledged to help him; and off they went (January 5, 1876) to do the only thing that could possibly help Costa, if only by showing their love for him. They knew, of course, that they might be laying down their lives for a friend.

Whether it was the unselfish motivation or a reward of Providence, these two accomplished the journey where they had failed before. They discovered a well-worn path, which not only shortened the distance but also permitted a much faster pace. They were back with us so soon that it was hard to believe they had been gone at all. But they returned empty-handed and morose. All of the barrels and boxes were where we had hidden them, but they were completely empty. The savages must have found the treasures and helped themselves to everything.

Now Costa's only hope was a miracle—a ship sighting, or even the reappearance of the black guardian angels. But it was not to be. Costa painfully and rapidly lost strength. He began to lose consciousness for brief periods and, on regaining it, when he struggled to speak to us was barely able to swallow the few drops of water we saved for him. And his voice sounded parched and faint: "Give me . . . give me some food." Fortunately, Dediol and I had a few berries, which we immediately offered him. With a feeble movement he tried to put them in his mouth but couldn't. He merely smeared them against his mouth and chin, as if anointing himself for death. I had witnessed the rite of Extreme Unction at home and had not forgotten the scene.

When he roused again with a final burst of strength, he spoke quite clearly and directly to me. "In a few seconds, Miho, I will be with God and I will plead for all of you, my dear friends." He fell back again, unconscious.

Before dawn (January 13), Lovrinovich awoke us with rather loud cries, which I felt must be the announcement of Costa's death. But Lovrinovich had just realized he had completely lost the sight in his left eye, which he had injured the night of the shipwreck. Thus awakened, I slowly approached Costa to ask how he felt. His glassy eyes staring toward heaven and the quiet of his body at rest answered my question. The shipwrecked captain had finally reached the peaceful harbor. "He's dead! He's dead!" I sobbed. All of the others quickly surrounded their departed guide and, one by one, kissed his hand. We said aloud, as best we could, the Office for the Dead.

And so for the fourth time, as dawn cleared the land, we dug a grave with nothing but our hands, this time about ten feet from the cave which had been our home. We laid him to rest shrouded in the few tatters left on his sorely bruised body and wound him in a part of the precious sheet he himself had sewn the first day ashore, nearly three months before!

A few days later, about January 17, we had a third encounter with the Aborigines. For all but two of us, it was to be the last such meeting. It also stands out in my mind for another reason. This time the natives seemed less concerned about our plight. We greeted them very enthusiastically but they, although pleasant enough, seemed preoccupied by their relentless push southward and kept on the move.

I nearly lost my precious shirt and trousers to the natives during this meeting. They were hanging on a bush to dry, and one of the men started to take them. I rushed toward him and indicated, mostly by gestures, how badly I needed the precious rags. He immediately returned them, with a wide grin, but kept for himself a spoon and some cord that he found in one of the pockets. While we were preoccupied, another native had entered our cave and fled with our most valuable possession—the flint for starting our fire!

The natives spent the next two days encamped at the nearby wells and then resumed their compulsive march south. Three of our men, Antoncich, Lovrinovich, and Brajevich, had spent the night with the Aborigines at the wells, in hopes of getting some food from them. They suddenly developed severe cramps and could not rejoin us when the natives left. For several days we walked the short distance, less than a mile, from the cave to the wells to care for them. Every visit found them weaker. Their morale seemed entirely gone, and they had almost no physical strength. We made less frequent visits. By now Dediol and Bucich had sickened as well; only Jurich and I were able to move about with any strength or vitality. Being younger and stronger made us fare slightly better, and both of us felt obliged to care for the others. However, care was limited to providing the bare essentials of water and a little food to the five helpless ones.

There were three major challenges that faced Jurich and me. First, we had a distance of about three-fourths of a mile to travel to the wells where Lovrinovich, Antoncich, and Brajevich lay disabled. Second, we had to keep the fire near the cave going constantly because of the flint being carried off. And finally, our daily search for food had become exhausting.

I was afraid neither of us had long to live under the circumstances. But I also thought our burden would become lighter as our less fortunate shipmates began to perish. One evening, on my trip to the well, I found Lovrinovich semiconscious, lying half in the well, muttering strange words. He was able to make me understand that he wanted to see his longtime friend and comrade Jurich before he died. So I hurried, as much as a half-dead boy could hurry, back to the cave to deliver Lovrinovich's last message. Jurich wasn't able to get to his companion until early the following day and found that the weary man had already died. It seemed so tragic that he died all alone, his last simple wish unfulfilled.

Two days later (January 23), when Jurich and I recovered from this shock, I came across the lifeless body of Brajevich stretched out on the ground near the path from the well to the shore. He had died, apparently, while struggling to return to the cave to be with Jurich and me. That same evening, when Jurich made his way back to the well for water, he found our only comrade who was still there barely breathing. There was just time for a glance of recognition before Antoncich was also gone. Terrified at this onrush of death that had taken three in the last three days, Jurich scurried back to the shore, pausing for just a second to remove a long woolen scarf from Antoncich's dead body. The poor soul had treasured it so much that only death could separate him from it.

It was not until the next day that Jurich and I could find the energy and will to bury our friends. Then we returned to the cave to try our best to care for Bucich and Dediol. It's hard to explain or understand our determination to see them through. The thought of being left all alone began to frighten me. I didn't want anyone else to die. We were somewhat encouraged because our task was now less tiring, and the four of us were in the cave together. With fewer mouths to feed and shorter distances to go, perhaps we could increase our food-gathering trips so we could slowly regain enough strength to try, once again, to walk to where we could be rescued or to where we could get food and water more easily. This possibility came too late for Bucich, who breathed his last the next day (January 25). Now there were only three of us—out of ten just a month ago.

For the first time I realized my main concern was to save myself. Jurich and I could still get around, but we were weakening noticeably. I regret to say we had given up on Dediol, who could barely move although he talked easily enough. We counted him as almost dead—maybe a couple of days more. I was already drawing up my plan for survival, and I knew it could work because I no longer had to think of the others. Jurich was equally capable of caring for himself; he could join me or not. I would feel free to do as I wanted, in any case.

I didn't know what was going on in Jurich's mind, but I assumed his thoughts were like mine. In spite of this ray of hope that was still buried somewhere deep inside, toward dark I became overwhelmed by an awful sense of despair. This was compounded by, or perhaps caused by, the most acute pains of hunger and thirst I had yet experienced. Jurich and I sat in the cave with Dediol, who lay beside the small fire. For hours we just sat there. Not a word, not a sound came from either of us. Not a tear came to our eyes. It was as if we had become petrified by the accumulation of horrors. I wished that my brain were as numb as my body because my thoughts had now become more painful than my limbs and empty stomach. I wondered why I was to die so young, so far from home. Why should there be such sorrow for my mother? How I missed my brothers and sisters! I wondered why I hadn't loved them more. I was too young for it to be too late. Jurich must have been experiencing the same agony as he sat leaning against the rocks.

After a night of horrible anguish filled with hallucinations I thought were dreams, the dawn came. I was glad I was still alive, but for the first time I feared death was only moments away. Bucich's body was the first thing I saw as light penetrated into the cave. Still unburied, the corpse with its staring, glassy eyes seemed to look into another world and then at me, in pity. Jurich was on the opposite side of the corpse, his eyes as fixed as mine. Suddenly, inexplicably, wildly, we fell on the corpse to devour it!

Dediol, who was still breathing, noticed our frenzy—the truth and horror of which came like a flash to his dying mind. He tried to raise his head. Turning toward us, he hissed more than uttered an awful curse: "May God damn your souls!" Then he fell back dead.

His curse, accompanied by his death, struck me like a lightning bolt. I was filled with shame and remorse. It appeared to affect Jurich the same way because we both slumped to the ground trembling and wept, until finally we regained control of ourselves. We didn't do anything all day—didn't eat and didn't drink. Bucich's body was still unburied, and the stench was now unbearable. I was aware that I had nearly committed a most grievous sin— cannibalism. Somehow, I didn't fear the pain of hell that surely awaited me in a few days when I would die. How could hell be any worse for me! As best I can recall, it was then I realized how strange it was that the first cannibal I encountered was myself.

If Jurich and I could get enough water, perhaps we could survive another day. He was suffering more than I and could just barely stand up. When I stood up, he begged me to make a trip to the well for water. I finally consented but only if he would let me have the last swallow of water we had in the water can. He agreed, and no sooner had I drained the very last drop than I told him, as I flung myself to the ground, that I could not and would not move a step. Jurich, infuriated by my shameless deception, found enough strength to rise and rush toward me to punish me with furious blows. But as we met, our strength ebbed, and we fended each other off until we emerged from the cave onto the beach. There we grappled weakly and then simply clenched each other. We fell to the ground, each hoping to gain some punishing advantage by using a headlock or leg lock on the other. For the whole day we struggled in the sand, pummeling each other with any stones or sticks in reach. Finally, toward the end of the day, we became locked together in our feeble combat—arms around neck, legs around waist, biting and clawing like the animals we had become. We collapsed to the ground exhausted and fell asleep.

The next morning, we were too weak to move, even to disentangle ourselves. So we just lay there on the sand while the rising sun punished both of us. We baked in the sun for hours, unable to move at all. Only brief periods of unconsciousness or sleep brought any comfort, and I hoped to die quickly. But the comfort of death was denied. At high noon, with the sun directly overhead, I again realized that I had sinned. This time it was deceit and dishonesty. I think I then recalled St. Peter, who sinned seriously three times in one day and was forgiven. Maybe it was this thought that allowed me to lose consciousness once again and find rest.

Toward evening I found myself praying before I really came to. I opened my eyes to a soft evening sky and saw an early-rising constellation, and around this heavenly vision was a ring of black faces. Even more beautiful than the stars were the eyes staring down with compassionate intensity. I—we—had been found by the fierce, savage cannibals of this wild land!

POSTSCRIPT: A few years later, two sightings of the "cave of death" were reported by eminent pioneers of the pastoral industry in the area. The first was by R. E. Bush, one of the earliest settlers on the Gascoyne River, who made an exploratory journey farther north in 1879. In his diary (which is held in the State Archives, Perth) he wrote:

*Sunday, November 16, 1879: On again, taking on
a young black fellow, and found a little water in a
rock at about 5 miles, the country improves here a
little.*

*The black fellows have a tale here, of a lot of white
people having been wrecked here years ago, and
showed us what looked like a grave of one, who had
died from eating a poisonous berry that grew here,
the way his mates buried him. We then made for
the beach again, and we found the bones of his comrades, who I suppose were frightened of leaving the
beach, for fear of the blacks, and the wreckage of a
boat that had been driven over the reefs. Well, we
buried these bones as decently as we could, in the
sand, could find no clue as to who they were, from
the bleached and rotten portions of dress lying
amongst the bones. We found them in a bit of a
cave, where they had crept to die from hunger, thirst,
little thinking that white hands would ever give their
remains some kind (however rough) of a burial. The
wild dogs had carried away a lot of their bones. We
covered their grave with fine big shells. If you only
saw the fearful reefs that these poor fellows must
have struggled to get over, they were fearful, the
worst I ever saw.*

The other pioneer was Thomas Carter, who was employed at
Wandagee sheep station when his work took him westward to the
coast early in 1889. He recorded in his diary:

*At Warroora was a limited supply of water—a soak,
in a sort of basin surrounded by rocks—and water
had to be carried up to the horses in a bucket and
emptied into a trough above, so watering took some
time. Brockman had been shearing there one year,
but loading the wool bales through the surf was so
difficult that boats would not call there again. In a
cave on the beach were the skeletons of some of the
crew of the Australian ship Stefanie [sic], which was*

wrecked at the Black Rock Channel at Point Cloates. Some of the crew wandered to Warroora, and no one ever knew if they died of starvation—which was most unlikely as the sea swarmed with turtle and fish, and there were turtle eggs and quantities of oysters all along the beach—or if the natives had killed them.

Later in the same year Carter took up a new pastoral lease centered on Point Cloates, where he built his house from ships' wreckage and relied heavily upon the Aborigines for labor. A noted ornithologist, in 1903 he published a comprehensive list of the birds of the area, recording the native names as supplied by the local tribe, the Talaindji.[1]

5

Life with the Tribe

The natives seemed to understand our peril, for they touched us gently and, with pitying looks, separated us from each other. We could barely move our lips, much less speak. Unable to stand, we crawled on the sand with much difficulty until our saviors, realizing the extent of our disability, carried us along the beach and past the unburied corpses of Bucich and Dediol. It was three-fourths of a mile to the plain with the familiar wells [Point F].

When we arrived, natives who were already camped there greeted us with joy and, more important, with food and water. We were somewhat restored. Our benefactors, taking care to allow space for our abdomens, which were distended from starvation, dug holes in the sand where we were to sleep.

The next day we were further improved, even though we were too feeble to walk much. We rested and ate and drank as much as we wanted. The men fished most of the day while the women and children gathered berries, fruit, and firewood. Periodically, they took some water to the men. Toward evening, when the men returned, they made it clear to us that they wanted us to stay with the tribe and go with them when they resumed their wanderings. We knew our basic needs were food and water, and they made us realize these would best be provided by them. I needed no convincing because this was the very plan I had had in mind for my survival when I decided I had to do something constructive if I didn't want to die like the rest. The only difference

48

was that I had planned to force myself on the natives. Jurich and I were equally happy to join the Aborigines, even though we knew it wouldn't be easy because they had to move far and fast each day in order to gather enough from the scant supply to keep from starving. We rested at the well-site meeting ground [Point E] for about a week. We were learning a lot about the daily routine of these people. Their needs were few; they were in perfect balance with nature. There was no surplus or waste, and although they occasionally went hungry, there didn't seem to be periods of famine.

I began to observe the evening rituals. As the only real meal of the day, the evening meal was the center of the natives' common activity. When the meal was ready the families, each group with its leader, came together. The men in each group sat with their backs to the women and ate first, then passed what was left over their shoulders to the women, who in turn distributed what remained to the children.

When supper was over, everyone prepared for the night by digging a sleeping space in the sand and by using branches and twigs to build a small windbreak to shelter their heads. Before retiring, the men gathered around various fires and began chanting mysterious words, which they accompanied by pounding on their weapons:

> *Paur paur gutari*
> *Puhur cerima*
> *Moli gumagura*

The ceremony lasted approximately an hour. Even after I learned the language somewhat, I never understood the meaning of the song or the ceremony.

Although fishing was the main source of food, the women's seed-gathering provided variety as well as quantity. At this location, the women gathered a bean somewhat like the European lentil. It was oblong and in pods that held twenty or more seeds. The pods grew on bushes that were three to four feet high and covered with long, slender, bright green leaves. The women dried the beans and ground them with stones. The resulting flour was immediately mixed with water and shaped into small loaves that were baked on hot embers. The bread had an unfamiliar taste, but I liked it and was always favored with a generous portion.

Something everyone relished was a species of seedless date, which was very sweet. It was never eaten raw but was roasted or baked. Only the women knew where to gather it, and they kept the location secret from the men of the tribe and from Jurich and me. I never received more than four or five small pieces and always craved more. One day after I had regained my strength, the men, with whom I had become very friendly, urged me to follow the women secretly to learn where they found the treasure. What a mistake! When the women discovered I was following them, they came after me and, with sticks and their fists, gave me a sound beating. The men, who had encouraged me, were greatly amused. While laughing, they teased me, *"Pignari cominini, pignari cominini!"* (Women are mean!)

As I began to learn their language, I noted that they seemed annoyed or irritated on hearing ours, especially when Jurich and I talked at length, as if they resented not knowing what we were saying. So we really tried to avoid long talks. We had benefited so greatly from their kindness, not only in sharing their food with us but also in befriending us and treating us like members of their tribe.

After we had rested a week, the tribe began preparations to move south. I recalled that it was February 3, the feast of St. Blaise (Sveti Vlaho), the patron saint of Dubrovnik. Jurich and I had expended considerable effort during the week of recuperation comparing our recollections and reconstructing the events following the shipwreck. (We later found our tally of days to be quite accurate.) Our realization it was a feast day at home brought other thoughts of home and a feeling of sadness. So we turned our thoughts to preparing for the forthcoming march.

The women had the important task of carrying fresh water. They carried it in crude wooden bowls that had been plastered on the outside with a paste of mud and grass to seal cracks. We knew we were to walk with the women and children, who traveled slowly, gathering seeds as they went. As we were leaving, I glanced back at the three fresh mounds of earth where the remains of Lovrinovich, Antoncich, and Brajevich lay, and I felt a great sadness. How lucky I was to be among the living. I knew that my new life as a nomad would be very hard, maybe more than I could manage, but there was no alternative other than death from starvation or thirst. I had high hopes of eventually being strong enough to try walking away to civilization, or at least to live long enough to sight and signal some heaven-sent sail.

The tribe took a roundabout way to Cape Farquhar [Point E], where we spent the night. The first day's march was very short, which was fortunate for Jurich and me because it was almost impossible to keep up, even with the women and children, and we were in pain.

Early the next morning, a small group of the men were anxious to move farther south in search of better fishing. Jurich and I were invited to go along. They kept repeating, *"Tataruga voteri."* We finally understood by signs that we were going fishing for turtles. A few women went along as water-carriers. We managed the day's walk satisfactorily and crossed a small brackish coastal lake [in the direction of Point G], ground which I had covered before, nearly three long months ago.

A curious thing happened that night. About midnight, wailing and wild shrieks broke the silence. Jurich and I were startled and rather frightened because we didn't know what it was, and we were the only ones who were concerned enough to get up. We eventually learned that the sounds came from a woman whose husband had disappeared sometime in the past few days. We remembered him and recalled that someone had said he was missing. No one seemed to care what had become of him. But one thing was certain. The tribe could not, or would not, stop their relentless life-supporting march. The mourner continued her lamentations for several nights. We realized how fortunate we were that this group of natives had waited so patiently for us, even at some risk to themselves.

The next morning brought early cries of *"Tataruga voteri,"* and turtle fishing started in earnest. At first, it seemed so easy. The natives detected turtles swimming near the shore or sleeping quietly on the surface. Before we even saw where a turtle was, a tribesman would jump into the sea and turn the turtle on its back. They also trapped turtles by setting nets near the shore to entangle the animals. Although it was hard work, our laughing friends treated it like fun and delighted in every capture. A captured turtle was immediately dragged on shore and beheaded. Certain innards were removed through the neck opening. The liver and other parts deemed delicacies were melted down and eaten first;

then the rest of the turtle was roasted still in its shell under a large mound of glowing coals. When the meat was half-cooked, it was easily removed from the shell, and the pieces of meat were placed directly on hot embers to finish cooking.

I was quite anxious to try this new food and found it very good, but my portion was much smaller than I had anticipated. When water became scarce, we turned north and, after one and a half days' march, rejoined the tribe near Cape Farquhar [Point E]. The entire excursion took three and a half days.

After a night's rest, our whole group pushed on to the other well site north of the cape [Point F].* It was only three to four miles away, and we arrived at noon. The women filled many water bowls, and the following morning we were off again, still heading north.

About midday we reached a large fertile plain, which appeared to be a meeting ground for neighboring tribes. There were fish-bones and other telltale remnants scattered around. The men built fires and prepared food but didn't touch a morsel until the women, carrying a lot of water, arrived in the evening. Although only ten days had passed since Jurich and I had nearly died in our battle on the sand, we had graduated from the women's group and were hunting and fishing with the men. Another short walk on the following day brought us to a fresh well, where we again prepared the food and waited several hours for the women to arrive.*

Every day we followed the same routine while constantly moving north: fishing, getting water, preparing food, eating, and sleeping—then getting up and repeating the routine the next day. Around February 9 or 10, we began to walk near the shoreline, even though the faint track was harder to travel than the well-worn paths inland. I was puzzled but not for long. Everyone was crying, "Majabulo, majabulo." A few moments later, to my astonishment, I saw two canoes in the bush ahead. The strange canoes had been hollowed out of some light tropical log and had carving at the bow. There was some bamboo trim and there was a partial shelter or decking. Judging by the material and the workmanship, I knew they were not products of our tribe but were

* Possibly Bulbarli Well, south of Warroora.
* Possibly Warroora Well.

probably the work of Malays, who I knew inhabited the thousands of islands above the North West Cape along the route to China.[†] The canoes were extremely light; two of the tribe carried them easily to the water. Bengo and Gjimmi, two heads of families in the tribe, took the boats out in deep rough water. They paddled them very fast and looked as if they were riding wild horses. Although this was an amusing distraction for Jurich and me, it did not take long for us to realize that these canoes might provide us the means to intercept some offshore sailing craft if any should pass by.

We decided to practice paddling and steering the canoes, but as often as we tried to get into the boat, it would tip over and give us a good dunking. One try followed another, always with the same result, and to the great amusement of the women and men who stood around us laughing uncontrollably and urging us to keep trying. We knew we would never be able to venture out in these bobbing corks. Besides, we got the impression that the craft were left in this spot for the use of various tribes who moved up and down this coast. After Jurich and I gave up dunking ourselves, Bengo and Gjimmi took the boats a short distance offshore and soon returned with two huge turtles, a grand meal for the tribe.

Whenever we moved on, we went whatever distance would take us to the next good source of fresh water, usually a full day's walk and sometimes farther. After three days in the place where we had found the canoes, we moved north again. We found wells that seemed to have been recently reopened and used by tribes that had preceded us. During our march, the natives kept repeating the phrase "Minara denki nagoru." Although I now had a fair vocabulary that included a number of useful phrases in the language, I could not decipher these words. From the solicitous tone in which the phrase was uttered and the fact that the words were always directed to Jurich and me, I decided that the natives anticipated something good for us. I was therefore anxious for some pleasant surprise. As our journey continued, the joy and exuberance of the natives increased, but I couldn't understand why. All I could do was smile and hope that perhaps there might be

---

[†] This was a good guess because many Malays were then in the pearling trade off the north coast of Australia and in Shark Bay. Many such small craft found their way along the coast.

some opportunity to be rescued. When we reached a large group of freshwater wells in the midst of another fine fertile plain [Point L, near Point Maud] and stopped for the night, it appeared that the tribe intended to remain awhile.‡ Some of the men drifted off as if to scout the area. Others went to the shore to fish. As always, everything seemed to await the arrival of the women. However, when they finally joined us, the waiting continued as if someone was still missing. It was hours before the mystery was solved by the arrival of another tribe—very large, loud, and friendly— which came from the north. This was about February 15.

Such wild shouts of welcome! Yelling, frantic gestures, laughing—it was indeed a special rendezvous between close friends who had not seen each other for a very long time. There were non-stop conversations in both small and large groups. Happy tales and, judging by tone and gestures, some sad ones, too, were being exchanged.

It became obvious that among the featured stories were tales of the wreck of the *Stefano*, the deaths of most of her crew, and the trials of the two poor survivors. This story must have touched the visitors because many of the new ones, especially the women, came over to Jurich and me and with sad faces touched us and gently kept repeating, "*Kaciujamoro*," which we took to be an expression of sympathy or, perhaps, words of encouragement.

Eventually the conversation slackened and then a chant like that of the past few days was taken up—"*Minara denki bolu*." Even the new natives were repeating it. Some of the men must have realized my frustration at not understanding because they seized my hands and Jurich's and led us—almost dragged us—to the nearby beach, where a strange but somewhat sad sight greeted us.

There was the lifeboat of the *Stefano*, securely stowed above high tide well up on the beach complete with several oars and a tattered sail. Crude repairs had been made to the sail, and the large hole in the side of the boat had been patched with matted grass and resin.

The boat must have been brought to this spot by natives who had found it farther north and were hoping to use it to fish for

‡ Possibly near Cardabia or Kooloobelloo Well.

turtles in this area. It was remarkable that they had found some of the oars we had lost. They had also found sailcloth, which they had repaired and rigged reasonably well.

Now the phrase I hadn't understood became clear to me. *Minara denki nagoru*—Shortly you will see your dinghy. The key word, of course, was *denki*, which I kept misinterpreting as an English corruption of *take it* or *thank you*. In fact, it was a more obvious derivation of the English word for a small boat, *dinghy*. (Jurich and I knew very little English then.) *Minara denki bolu* meant "soon you will sail your dinghy," and sure enough, that was the plan for morning.

I was too excited to have a restful sleep that night. The events of the day—the large gathering and reunion, and the sight of the boat, which had brought Costa and me safely to shore—stirred up too many vivid memories. But most of all, I was concerned that abandoning the lifeboat was a mistake that might have cost eight lives!

The little training I had had repeatedly stressed that the lifeboat is the sailor's one hope in any tragedy at sea. More than once I had thought about shipmates' tales of long journeys in small boats that were crowded with survivors.*

But, with some measure of defensiveness, I reasoned that our situation had been different. The boat had a large hole in it. Also, we had very little water available right after the wreck. And yet the Aborigines had repaired the hole and we had eventually discovered water. Why hadn't we stayed with the boat or returned to it later to try to use it in our attempt to survive?

The most depressing thought was that the lifeboat, had we repaired it, would clearly have been the easiest and quickest way to get to the Gascoyne River from Point Cloates. We would probably have been able to make it seaworthy by using material and

---

* In this part of the globe there have been some very remarkable instances. A lifeboat from the Dutch ship *Batavia* carried the shipwrecked survivors from the west coast of Australia to Java in 1629. In 1789, Captain Bligh was set adrift with eighteen men in a small open boat from H.M.S. *Bounty* and sailed the craft from the Tonga Islands to Timor 3,600 miles in forty-one days, with no lives lost. When the American ship *Rapid* was wrecked off Point Cloates in 1811, a few miles from where the *Stefano* was lost, the captain and twenty-two men sailed three small yawl boats to Batavia, Java, in forty-five days.

tools found in the wreckage. A trip by boat would probably have taken about three days. The distance was only one hundred and twenty miles, and the prevailing onshore wind—out of the west—would have enabled a southerly heading to be easily maintained. Moreover, the almost continuous offshore reef from one to three miles out would have provided calm, sheltered waters for a short journey. I was quite angry with myself by now and was tempted to remind Jurich that all of us had made a serious error of judgment, but nothing would be gained by upsetting him. Eventually I realized we could now use the boat to sail north to our original campsite, which could be no more than fifty miles away. Once there, we could make more substantial repairs to the boat, fill some of the abandoned empty casks with water, and sail to the Gascoyne River in about three days' time. This was something I would discuss with Jurich.

Very early the next morning, the natives took us for a sail. We stepped the mast and rigged the sail and took the five oars with us. After a successful launching, nothing went right. No one took charge; there were eight of us with different ideas in mind. The rigging parted, the aged sail gave way, and the hull leaked. We furled the sail and tried to row. The oars jumped out of the rowlocks because of defective rowlocks and poor oarsmanship. So we gave up good-naturedly without even trying to go after turtles. There were still several that hadn't been cooked the previous night that could serve for the day's meals.

That evening the same mysterious verse was sung at bedtime; even the new tribe knew it well, but not even our closest friends in the tribe could explain it. No one knew exactly what the words meant, but they did say the song was very old!

By morning I had definitely decided not to reveal any of the plans I had had for the lifeboat. It wasn't just because of the disappointing performance of the boat that morning; it was primarily my reluctance to part company with the wonderful people who had been so good to me.

If I had only known then what I was to discover later, I would not have hesitated a moment to put my entire salvation in their hands. Without our knowledge, they had been working conscientiously on a plan for our rescue that was beyond anything required or expected.

Early that day, February 19, the two tribes decided to separate and proceed on their journeys. There was no question in Jurich's or my mind that we would continue with our original group whom we now knew so well. Thus, it came as a surprise when some of the senior men came to us and said, *"Bullura vagaj,"* meaning "go ahead," as they motioned to the tribe moving to the north. I was inclined to join the group because they were going north, and the tip of the North West Cape still seemed to provide the best chance for sighting passing ships. Also, the new group seemed to be more successful in catching fish and gathering food. But my emotional ties to the first tribe were too strong for me to want to leave them.

Before we could make a decision, it was made for us. An old man from our tribe shouted to the departing natives, *"Vac-balla gindara go ota!"* (Wait for the whites!) The tribe stopped short, and Jurich and I, not sure that this would really be our last meeting, bade quick and sad farewells to our benefactors.

The new tribe, about a hundred people, was much larger than the old. For five consecutive days we were on the march at a pace we weren't accustomed to and with barely any stops for rest. We followed paths that went in all directions, although it seemed our overall movement was north.

Jurich began to suffer the effects of this new routine and collapsed several times. I was traveling with another part of the tribe some distance away. Those accompanying him sent two men to find me. When I reached him, I noticed that the entire tribe had stopped, somewhat bewildered at this new encumbrance, but it was clear no one would move on until Jurich had recovered. We had little expected such consideration from these strangers. Our march resumed reasonably soon and we moved more slowly the next two days. To my surprise, we arrived once again at the communal meeting place [Point Maud—Point L], where the two tribes had spent the days of celebration. Most of our old tribe had gone on their way and the boat was no longer there. We were puzzled to find we had been walking mostly in circles, or back and forth, for over a week. Later, I was to understand this mystery. But for the present, a strange thing happened. The two tribes, previously so friendly, seemed to have a disagreement, and before long, tempers rose and the men became unbelievably furious with each other. The two groups assembled at the bottom of a large hill, and one tribe climbed to the top, hurling shouts and curses at those below. Eventually, the air was full of flying weapons like some scene from Dante.

Jurich and I were horrified and we feared for our safety, so we fled to the beach, where the women and children had already sought sanctuary. At first the women seemed unconcerned but then they became alarmed, constantly repeating to us, "Bulac-balla pignari." (Our men are too hostile.) Finally they could no longer stand the combat. About a dozen of the older women ran to the hill and threw themselves into the fray and demanded that it stop. The victory was theirs, and a total one, too. All laid down their weapons and rejoined their families to have their wounds and bruises tended. There were no fatalities or even serious injuries. Those who hadn't fought were the most injured. No food had been gathered or prepared, and hunger had returned. Many of the men had wandered off, and we didn't know what to expect next.

Some days later, about March 1, a few stragglers appeared on the crests of hills in the distance and gradually a few more figures appeared. The women were elated and sang out, "Bulac-balla nagaru." (Our men are coming back.) Slowly the men came down from the hills, looking somewhat embarrassed and at times scowling. They began to gather the boomerangs and spears that were scattered about. Then slowly, reluctantly, they moved to the beach. Men from both tribes gathered.

It was a remarkable scene to witness. The men made peace with each other, exchanging apologies and reaffirming their affection, without any restraint. Then they began boasting about how many blows each had sustained without ill effect. Later, they explained to the women where they had been in the meantime—far into the interior to gather the much treasured food, the tasty palm date,* as a peace offering. They had brought back a large quantity, which were roasted and served to all. Following the light meal, all of the men and most of the women went fishing or to gather food. Left behind with Jurich and me were two very old men of the new tribe, who were obviously over sixty years old, and two women who appeared to be in their eighties.

After four or five hours, everyone returned. The men carried

---

* Cicas redlei, according to Father Skurla in the original manuscript.

a lot of fish of differing sizes, but all of the same variety. As usual, family groups gathered and started cooking fires. Soon two happy tribes sat down to a welcome supper. This bountiful and peaceful day was followed by two equally fine days which gave us the opportunity to observe the differences between the two tribes, and the opportunity to make some new friends. Jurich and I discovered two who were to become our guardians and bene-factors—Gjaki and Gjimmi. The latter, who was about thirty years old and head of an old woman's family, became Jurich's close friend. As was the custom, the old woman carried water for Gjimmi and prepared his food. In some way they were related, and the two lived in a small family group with a childless old couple.

Jurich was indeed fortunate to have such a fine friend because he had for some time been suffering from ulcers and sores all over his shoulders, caused by sunburn, and his legs and feet had been cut by sharp rocks and rough grass. For days, Gjimmi carefully dressed Jurich's wounds with a mixture of moist clay and sand until finally all wounds were healed.

The most important blessing of our new friendship was the sharing of food, which was always generously offered to us, even when the supply was scarce. We had many reasons to be thankful.

6

The Last Walkabout

On the morning of March 5, many of the company prepared for what it seemed would be another long march to the north. There were about a hundred people in all; most were from the second tribe. At last it appeared we would be on our way to the tip of the North West Cape, which I thought to be less than one hundred miles away.

During the second period with the two tribes, I pieced together bits of information, observations, and some speculation and came to an understanding of the mysterious behavior of the tribes over the previous two weeks—why our attempt to move on with the new tribe was aborted and the reason for the quarrel that occurred on our return.

Shortly after we joined the first tribe, the leaders of the group had decided they must help us be rescued or we would surely die. It was impossible for them to keep us with them indefinitely because we prevented them from traveling rapidly, and we upset the balance between the tribe and its supply of food and water. I discovered later that the senior men thought if they could get us back to the *Stefano*'s dinghy, beached about thirty miles away, we would be able to sail away to civilization. This was not an unreasonable conclusion because during their lives they had seen numerous small boats appear from beyond the horizon, sailed with apparent ease by white men. That is why they were so excited and kept repeating, "Shortly you will see your dinghy." But, clearly, that plan had failed because the dinghy was not in good enough condition. Nor did it seem that we young men could handle it well enough.

As I learned more and more of their language and customs, it also came to my attention that the site where the dinghy was stored, Point Maud, not only was the meeting ground for several tribes, but also was the boundary line between the territories of the north and south tribes [Point L on the map]. The boundary line was very important. Even though the tribes were closely related by blood and through marriage, their territorial boundaries defined the areas in which each had exclusive rights to hunt, fish, and gather food. During the large community reunion and feasting two weeks earlier, the southern tribe, our first friends, sought permission to continue beyond the boundary line to deliver Jurich and me to the North West Cape, where ship sighting was most frequent and where rescue was most likely. This arrangement was apparently not agreed to.

However, the northern tribe did agree to let us join them to be taken to the North West Cape as a part of their normal journey. As has already been explained, the southern tribe had urged us to go ahead without them and then insisted on it. When the new tribe returned us within a week, it was because we proved more of a burden than they had anticipated. The fight which followed was the result of our original black friends demanding that we must be helped by the tribe from the north.

As it happened, there was a reasonable compromise. The northern tribe agreed to take us with them so long as a small group from the south went along to care for us in case we should fall behind or become ill. Gjaki and Gjimmi were appointed or volunteered to be our guardians.

For nine consecutive days, we proceeded without any rest except at night. We were just not able to keep up with the new pace. The food supply also dwindled because of the continuous march. We had to gather shellfish—crayfish—from the shore as we walked. At one time we could hardly drag ourselves along and were falling behind. The natives tried to encourage us (or challenge us) by repeating, *"Bullura vagaj!"* (Let us go ahead, or Keep moving!) We mistakenly thought *bullura* meant "cape" because the natives were so anxious to get us there. I asked, *"Vangi bullura?"* because I wondered where the cape was, but I was actually asking, "Where is ahead?" The answer was always, "*Parue, parue*" (Faraway, faraway)—an appropriate answer to either question.

In addition to our physical suffering, we were in for an emotional blow. When Lovrinovich had made his long treks to recover material from our then distant old camp, he told of a boat he had discovered beached high on the shore. On the fourth day of our march we came upon it [Point M] about halfway between Point Maud and Point Cloates. It appeared to be of English construction, about fifty feet long and in poor condition. It was probably wreckage from the cyclone of December 24, which had also taken the lives of our shipmates Perancich and Vulovich.

Three days later, we came upon the very spot where our first camp had been pitched, slightly south of Point Cloates [Point B]. The natives, knowing its significance, slowed down and then stopped completely, enabling us to look it over and recall it with sadness. The hut made of lumber and sailcloth was all there, just as we had left it, but the provisions and other hidden articles had all been discovered and taken, except for a large container of potatoes. Naturally, they were now spoiled. I wondered why Lovrinovich hadn't found them when he came in early January looking for food. I stared blankly at the shelter, then at the ground and the sky; and my eyes filled up. I could no longer hold back my tears. I wept as our black companions gathered around to console me.

As we left, I discovered by chance a caseful of needles. I was delighted because I knew it could prolong the life of the rags I was wearing. I sought to hide it in my rags, but one of the sharp-eyed women noticed, and she ran up to snatch it away. I refused to part with it and this started an unexpected commotion. Everyone urged me to give her the needles, but I refused. I had no idea what she would do with needles. The natives wear no clothes whatsoever and have no thread. No matter! She wanted them and everyone seemed to side with her. Some compromise was necessary, so I suggested I would exchange one needle for something of value. Her husband, immediately grasping the notion of barter, offered about a pound of crayfish, which was beyond my usual ration, and the exchange was made! The needle was now the proud possession of the man's wife. I realized I had a wonderful fortune that could be exchanged for food when the supply was particularly limited.

The tribe evidently had a certain location in mind for the next resting place. For the first time we walked through most of the night without even pausing to eat. The following day we were overtaken by a few men from the southern tribe. I wondered how they could catch up so fast. I learned they had followed an inland track and carried prepared food and water in order to avoid stopping to fish and cook.

That night none of us really enjoyed our meal, which consisted of two large rayfish (skates), one fat lizard, and four snakes. We were obviously in poor country for fishing or food gathering. Before eating, I checked to make sure the two pet snakes the tribe carried with them were still accounted for. Satisfied, I tried the new foods, which weren't too bad, given that we were so hungry.

The natives predicted rain for March 11 and the next two days, and they were right. There was a great deal of thunder and lightning. One native pointed to the top of a mountain in the distance and explained that Giunovagnabari, their chief god, was angry and would continue to hurl lightning and thunder down on us. I had the native join me under the shelter of sailcloth as the rain fell hard.

Several days later, March 15 (the Ides, I believe), the Aborigines decided to divide into separate groups to approach the cape from slightly different routes, both going north. Jurich went with the first group, and shortly after, I left with the second. It was a beautiful, calm day after the rain. The calm was suddenly shattered by cries of "Jamina, jamina!" I wondered what was going on and, ever curious, had to find out. After being scolded for noisiness, I tiptoed toward the long line of men and women strung out along the higher dunes which overlooked the shore. When I got there, a friend nudged me and pointed to a huge sea monster swimming slowly toward shore.

Like a small army, the little band of black men hurried to battle. A long line formed and moved closer and closer to the water's edge. Some of the tribe stayed on higher ground to keep sight of the strange creature. Others climbed the nearest tall hill and quickly got a smoke fire going to alert the first tribe, which was a mile or so ahead, to our situation. This call for help was almost immediately answered; they came running. About forty of the best men were lined up along the water's edge, each watching the prey and waiting with a club, stone, or spear for exactly the right moment to strike. In an instant, with fierce yells, the entire line plunged into the water, carrying with it a large net-like snare that I had not previously noticed. They were quick to encircle the animal, which seemed to be seeking the refuge of the bottom. One native after another dived toward the beast to deliver deadly blows. It would rise to the surface momentarily and plunge down again in a swirling eddy, carrying black men with it, only to reappear a few moments later in a renewed struggle. At last, mortally wounded by the stones and other weapons, the huge creature was dragged ashore.

The animal was the dugong, an herbivorous mammal frequently found in the tropical waters of the East Indian seas, particularly in the shallow waters of bays and beyond the reefs where marine vegetation abounds.[†] The flesh is highly prized as food, and the blubber provides a clear, much desired oil. Dugongs range in size from ten to twenty feet long, and this one was close to maximum size. This was, indeed, manna in the desert, and the feast began. First the delectable organs—liver, spleen, etc.—were removed and eaten raw! Next the head and tail were cut off but were not discarded. Then the meat was carefully removed from the bones and sliced into serving-size portions for the families, which patiently and politely waited their turn. There must have been some preexisting order to this ritual because everyone—from the fishers to the butchers to the oldest men and women who had taken no part in the capture—knew what to expect and what to do. The hot embers were soon ready and the ravenous crowd was fed. The leftover uncooked portions were cut up for easier handling, and it looked as if there would be enough for several more days. We remained at that spot for three more days, until March 20. The drinking water was very brackish because it came from a hole dug near the shore. No one wanted to leave the site of such rare fare merely to get fresh water. The water was too salty to swallow and by now the uncooked meat was beginning to smell bad. By

---

[†] A close relative of the manatee, which is found in the rivers and off the coast of Florida. As a protected endangered species, the manatee is now making a slow comeback.

the next day even the rancid dugong meat had been devoured, so we went along the coast until we came to a well with fresh, clear water that tasted so good we stayed the rest of that day and the next.[‡]

An unfortunate incident occurred that night. It gave me further insight into the nature of my native companions. In a very atypical act, a middle-aged man began quarreling with his wife and lost all control of himself. He beat her mercilessly until she fell bleeding and semiconscious to the ground. I was terrified to witness the beating. The other men were also horrified at the sight, and they gathered around the offender, seized him, and beat him until he begged for mercy. He was forced to be reconciled with his wife and both were required to smear their heads with a thick white paste of powdered shell, evidently a badge of shame. The tribal response to the incident is only one of many I recall that illustrates the attractive character of these simple people.

The capture of the dugong and the subsequent feast had brought the two parts of the tribe together, and we decided to travel that way for a while. We still had a long way to go to reach the tip of the cape. I figured we were about halfway there. On March 24, we left the well, and once again Jurich and I were obliged to walk with the women. Neither of us could keep up. We had to carry water containers—humiliating, but fair. What upset me was that my constant companion on the walk was an old woman who must have been eighty years old, and I could barely keep up with her. My pride was restored somewhat the following day when I was given weapons to carry. I wore them, rather than just carried them, and imagined myself to be a fierce warrior.

About sundown, as I scanned the sea's vast horizon out of habit rather than expectation, I was startled and, for a moment, stunned. I started wildly waving a piece of cloth I snatched from a woman's shoulders and began shouting toward the sea. This was the very first time since the day of the wreck—five months earlier—that I had sighted a ship. Barely a mile away there was a full-rigged schooner moving farther away every second. My voice was hoarse, but I kept screaming even though I knew full well that I couldn't be heard. The ship grew indistinct and I became numb with de-

‡ Probably the large waterhole which still exists a mile north of Sandy Point, about seven miles south of Yardie Creek.

spair. In frenzy and ecstasy, I kept this up for a few minutes, and when I stopped, I glanced toward heaven in despair and sobbed, "It is gone!" My old friend came and patted me on the back to show her sympathy, but I hardly saw or heard her as she tried to give me some courage. I finally came out of my stupor and ran ahead in search of Jurich to tell him what had happened. Although Jurich hadn't seen the sail, he was encouraged by the news of the sighting. We were certainly nearing the right location from which to hail a ship. And I had already sighted the first.

We weren't quite ready to stop for the night. A rather prominent gully cut across our path along the coast, just beyond a marshy spot where small bushes were growing in the water. We stopped for the night on the near side of this slough and waited for morning to cross the long inlet of the sea. We decided to wade across the forty to fifty feet, rather than walk the considerable distance inland to get around the inlet. The blacks waded straight ahead with no concern about the sharp shells and slippery bottom. Jurich and I followed, but we slipped and fell several times, much to the amusement of our agile friends. Finally we plunged in and began swimming European-style. The remainder of the natives followed us in grotesque but good-humored imitation.*

That evening, after another meal of stingray, Jurich came down with severe stomach cramps. His moans and groans carried throughout the encampment. He had previously suffered a severe toothache and nothing we did brought any relief until Cialli, the tribe's healer, with a few words and a little ointment cured him completely. We called for Cialli again, but this time his treatment had no results. So he tried a new method. Taking hair from Jurich's head, he moistened it with oil from the ray and rubbed the hair over Jurich's abdomen. The patient was soon relieved— whether from the rubbing, the oily hair, or his imagination we knew not—and cared not.

Four days later and farther north, we had to cross another inlet. This one was about the same width as the previous one but deeper. It could be crossed only by swimming.* This time my faithful provider Gjaki, an excellent and strong swimmer, insisted that I

* This was probably Yardie Creek (Point P), the most prominent inlet on the shore between Point Cloates and the North West Cape, about forty miles south of the cape.
* Probably Pilgonaman Creek, ten miles north of Yardie Creek.

cross on his shoulders. On the other side we discovered a large plain [Point Q on the map] and a well with clear fresh water—the best we had had in a very long time.[†]

Before sundown some of the women went into the bush. They did not return until the next morning. They brought back a great number of insects that resembled Mediterranean honeybees. The women showed me the hives, made from soft wet mud which hardened as it baked in the hot sun. The hives were about five feet high and three feet wide at the base. Each tapered-cone shape was pierced with tiny holes which gave it a rough exterior. I watched the women gather the insects by placing smoking fire-brands around the hives; the smoke made the insects docile victims.[‡]

On March 30, we wandered onto a sandy plain [Point R]. It stretched in all directions as far as the eye could see, and there were no shrubs, not even a single blade of grass. We stopped near the shore for the night. Some of the men silently left as I was falling asleep. In the morning they showed me the reward of their night's labor—ten large turtles. One of the natives, showing me his fingers, said with pride, "Nulla villa tataruga dadalgo." (We have taken as many turtles as I have fingers.)

I was glad we left this spot after two days because the heat was becoming more intense as we moved north, and the barren sand of this spot with no shade seemed to multiply the burning effects of the sun. One morning, a day or so later, Jurich and I threw ourselves into the surf to seek some refuge from the sun. Our black friends, noticing this, rushed in after us. Aware of our discomfort, they got us out of the water, made us stretch out on a cool strip of damp sand, and gave us a wonderful, relaxing massage from head to toe. As physically recuperative as this treatment was, it had a greater emotional effect. Hardly a day went by without some gesture of this kind, their reaching out to us from the greatness of their gentle souls. My admiration of these simple people continued to grow. As the recollection of our "civilized" behavior of just a few weeks ago came back to disturb me, I found myself wondering who were the savages.

[†] Probably Pilgonaman Well, still shown on topographic maps.
[‡] A rather accurate description of termites or flying ants and their hills, but not honeybees!

I was jolted out of my meditation by a crisis. Loud, dolorous cries arose from the midst of the tribe—the cries of a poor mother who for the past few days had been watching over her sick child. The unfortunate one had drawn its last breath. The sorrow and lamentations of the grieving parents quickly became the sorrow and lamentations of the entire tribe, and everything else halted as, one by one, each native gently embraced and patted the afflicted parents. Meanwhile, Cialli, the tribe's physician, took upon himself the role of chief mourner. He retired into the bush and soon returned with his head and torso covered with green foliage and small branches and twigs. The women, on seeing him, begged him to come among them and mourn for the untimely death of the young one.

Meanwhile, funeral preparations were progressing. The parents of the dead child, in what I suspect was a gesture of grief or sacrifice, threw into the sea the fish they had saved from the precious catch. Nearby, a huge fire was started and it quickly became a deep bed of glowing coals.

Somehow, I sensed what was about to happen even though not a word was spoken. The child's corpse was laid atop the glowing coals. All of us gathered around the pyre. Quickly and mysteriously, I realized that this was not to be a cremation. The young one was being roasted for a gruesome meal.

It began with the first portion being offered to the father, who had gone alone to the top of a nearby hill. The mother was served next as we all sat around the dying embers. Then everyone else was served until the small corpse was completely consumed.

After the feast, the bones were gathered with a semblance of religious ritual and devotion. I found myself participating in the ceremony without the slightest hesitation or any thought of impropriety. The fact that I was automatically included by the natives made me acutely aware of the bond of brotherhood that existed between us. I seemed to have as much of a need to console as the parents had to be comforted. And as I joined in the ritual on the barren shore of the Indian Ocean that evening, I felt puzzlement and mystery. I partook of something very serious which I did not fully understand, but which I somehow knew was completely appropriate.[1]

The next morning the grieving father arose and led the tribe, in total silence, on the continued trek to the north. Toward day's end, he stopped the group at a shallow depression near the shore where an abundance of clamshells had been deposited by the waves. The natives gathered a quantity of shells, crushed them, ground them into fine white powder, and mixed it with water. The thick paste was smeared over the heads, arms, and chests of the dead child's parents until they were hideously white. Then the rest of the natives smeared paste over themselves, except the married women, who put the white paste only on their hair. This was not to be the end of the ceremonies. For the next ten nights, shortly before dawn, all of the married women would arise and join the bereaved mother in chanting the most doleful choruses, among them a most beautiful, although heartbreaking, dirge "Cai-biri gogoj curi." (O young one, return to unfortunate me.)

For several days following the requiem feast, I was troubled by doubts about my behavior, especially when I recalled my religious instruction. Cannibalism had been described as a sacrilege, the most serious kind of sin. I could not recall the reasons, given the Church's teaching that we Christians should regularly consume the body and blood of Christ. Even so, I decided that I would try to be more loyal to civilized European traditions in the future. Later the same day, a brave hunter managed to catch and kill a wild dog using only stones for weapons. The next day, while the men were fishing, the women roasted the dog for the evening meal. Because I was tired of the constant diet of turtles and fish, I begged them for a small portion of the animal. I was not only quickly refused but chased away with violence. When the fishermen returned, I complained to them about this incident. They calmly explained, "Vac-balla mira vangia bagialgo!" (White men do not eat dogs!)

7

Exmouth

The next day (April 4) the northward march resumed. We walked for three full days, barely stopping even to sleep. For the most part, we were spread out in little groups. On the third day we turned inland toward an inviting grassy plain to the east. As we moved in this new direction, the ground, still damp from recent rain, became pleasantly cool underfoot. Suddenly, on reaching high ground, we saw the ocean ahead of us to the east. It then became obvious that the North West Cape was, in reality, a peninsula, tapering here at its northern extremity. We crossed to the opposite shore below the tip and came to a pleasant spot which the natives called Bundegi.*

About a mile inland, before we reached the eastern shore, we came across a sizable well. It seemed deeper than previous wells and had been more carefully dug, its opening shored with sticks and branches. An unexpected feature was an inverted barrel thrust into the opening to protect and cover the well. I thought it was surely the work of white men and felt encouraged by signs of white men's presence. At that time only three or four of the tribe were with me. In unison they told me, "*Nulla vac-balla, Carcara*

---

* Current maps show Bundegi reef at this location on the Exmouth Gulf, about thirteen miles south of the northern tip of the peninsula. It is a three-mile-long formation about a half mile offshore.

villa babba." I took their reference to *Carcara* to mean a European settlement whose settlers had dug the well.*

Jurich, who was with another small band, had walked along the western shoreline and crossed over to the opposite side of the cape just below the tip of the cape [Point T]. Near the northern point was the wreckage of a very large schooner, high on a reef and rather close to shore. It didn't seem to be an old wreck because it wasn't badly weathered. On the stern was the name *Fairy Queen—Singapore*.† There were quantities of small wreckage in somewhat ordered piles on the beach—a great many coconuts, empty bottles, broken chests, ship's implements, and an immense rusty anchor with some lengths of chain. Jurich had questioned the natives about this curious collection of salvage and finally, with considerable difficulty, learned that the white men had, some way or other, asked the natives to gather as much wreckage as they could so another ship could call to pick it up and reward the tribes for their efforts. Here again was an indication that this area was a crossroads where whites met up with blacks.

Igrana, a giant black fellow, added to Jurich's optimism when he told him, *"Minara Cialli gogoj Pulimandur vagaj, ciullu bagialgo ciugga turaggi bagialgo, thie bagialgo coconagi bagialgo."* (In a little while Cialli returns, you will go to Pulimandur, and you will eat much sugar, rice, tea, and cocoa.) But Jurich was practical in reporting this to me, reminding me that we dare not base our hopes on these words because he was convinced that the natives were talking about survivors of the wreck who had evidently been rescued under circumstances much different from ours.

Jurich and I were reunited when the small groups came together near Bundegi [Point S] and headed south as a whole. This troubled

---

* *Carcara* is probably another phonetic spelling of what is now commonly *Karrakatta*, which was the native name for Mount Eliza and the vicinity, the site of the city of Perth. The tribesmen were evidently indicating that white men from Perth had dug the well (literally, "White men here, water how it is in Perth"). There can be little doubt the well was the work of men hailing mainly from the metropolitan townships who had come north in recent years to engage in either pearling or whaling. The well was still in existence in 1987 and is shown on current topographic charts as Cape Well, about one mile inland from Bundegi reef.
† Lately purchased in Singapore to work the pearling grounds, the schooner *Fairy Queen* was wrecked at the cape in August 1875 without loss of life.

me somewhat because we had struggled so long to reach this northern apex. I feared it wasn't wise to leave, especially with so many signs of white men's periodic presence.

But by this time, Jurich and I had strong faith in our friends and firmly believed that they would see to our rescue. So we went along with them without protest or question. The next three days were difficult for the two of us. The bush and foliage came down close to the eastern shore and there was no apparent track. Even so, women with water bowls on their heads moved with as much celerity as the men. We could barely keep up with them, and once again our limbs were cut and bruised. It had been nearly six months since we came ashore, but we still had not accustomed ourselves to the harsh environment. Luckily, on the third day, our arrival at a fine clearing near the shore brought the tribe to an early stop and gave us two pleasant days to rest [Point U].

Something strange occurred during this rest. The water here was not taken from still wells but had to be collected from swirling creeks that coursed toward the shore.‡ The task of collecting water appeared to be dangerous. The men wouldn't permit the women to do their usual chore. Instead, only the men drew water for the two days we were there. Could it be that these savage men were also somewhat chivalrous?

April 12 found us again on the trail. This time Jurich and I were obliged to carry water bowls on our heads. We were not well suited to the task. Presently Vallero, an unusual black who never did any work, came to my rescue. He relieved me of my heavy container of water and easily carried it under his huge arm for the rest of the day's journey.

This man Vallero was an extraordinary person. He was so tall that the next tallest man in the tribe barely reached his shoulders. His body was big in all respects, and he was not proportioned the same as the other natives. He had a full bosom that rivaled the women's in size, and his enormous abdomen hung over his hips. There were other peculiarities that strongly suggested he was of another race. There was a total absence of beard or other body

‡ Evidently rain showers in the high ridge of hills to the west caused the normally dry creek beds to fill. Such creek beds are plentiful along the coast from Bundegi to the Bay of Rest.

hair, and the hair on his head was very stubby. He was unlike anyone else in the three tribes. I estimated him to be forty years old. The entire tribe looked on him with devotion and, to a degree, veneration. Everyone waited on him, and he was never assigned any duties. I speculated that he, too, many years ago, might have been a castaway like us. Perhaps he was an African, a slave, or in ship's service, or perhaps he was from a New Guinea tribe, people who resemble Africans in size and features.

Our tribe had not traveled very far that morning when some scouts gave a cry which was passed up and down the marching line, "*Tanic-balla jurogaja!*" (The ship is nearing!) This was all it took for Jurich and me to break from the ranks and rush to the shore to see what was happening. One of the oldest men, Cagiaro, had already climbed the nearest high hill to light an enormous bonfire that must have been visible for miles seaward. Many of the rest of us scrambled up the hill to join the old man. We stood motionless staring at the horizon in hopes of seeing the long-desired sight. And there at the north end of Exmouth Gulf, just barely visible to the naked eye, was a full-rigged sloop! I wondered what a white man's ship would be doing in this barren area with an entire coastline surrounded by coral reefs and treacherous shallows between the reefs and shore. This ship, as if it heard my thoughts, seemed to move seaward, avoiding any approach to the gulf. Minutes seemed like hours as Jurich and I experienced the tortures of Tantalus. But as soon as it became clear to us that the ship was rounding the tip of the cape and heading into the Indian Ocean, we both let loose with loud screams, curses, and blasphemy. The uncharacteristic display revealed how painful and frustrating was our despair. The natives, ever true to their character, overwhelmed us once again with their sympathetic, comforting words and gestures.

By now I was quite tired of their constant references to Cialli and Pulimandur. "*Minara Cialli daghi Pulimandur vagaj.*" (Soon Cialli will come and you will leave for Pulimandur.) As my annoyance increased, I tried to ignore my friends, lest I respond in a way I would later regret. And it was good that I exercised such self-control because I would soon understand the simple meaning of all those strange words. *Pulimandur* was a phonetic corruption of Fremantle, the chief port on the western coast. Likewise, the oft-repeated *Cincin* was Tien Tsin,* the nearest port on the northern coast, some two hundred miles to the east. But even after learning this, I could not figure out an appropriate meaning for *Cialli*. Where was it? What could it be? I was not even close to realizing that it was the name of our savior-to-be, the nearest the natives could come to pronouncing "Charlie."

Somehow, Jurich was beyond self-restraint. As we watched the tiny white ship disappear, one of the women crept up behind him and ladled water out of his container into hers. My despondent shipmate, without reflecting, grabbed the nearest weapon, a flat spear, and beat the poor woman so fiercely over the shoulders and head that she fell to the ground. "My God, what have you done?" I shrieked. It was a despicable act and I instantly recalled the punishment meted out for such abuse. The native men quickly gathered around to hear the witnesses' account of what had happened.

Whether it was the nature of the account or the nature of the men in charge, Jurich received nothing for his unforgivable abuse but silent stares and painful looks. For the rest of the day and throughout the night, I was tormented by thoughts of the incident. I felt we must apologize and ask forgiveness. I couldn't give a second thought to the boat sighting or the prospects of rescue when I knew that we had seriously offended our friends and providers.

My brooding must have been very obvious, for early the next morning several men and women, including my closest friends, met with us to explain, to our great humiliation, that one may tease the women, play tricks on them, or even curse them, but one may not use physical force—a lecture on manners in the wilderness. And then all was forgiven. Nothing more was ever said or done.

A few days later, April 15, to be exact, I was back to my habit of chronic horizon-watching. My eyes hardly left the sea for a moment that day. Suddenly I spied a sail and sped off to Jurich with the good news. By now he had become quite stoic and found little hope or joy in this new sighting. Nevertheless, we both ran to the shore, where we again willingly set ourselves up for the

---

* Tien Tsin was later renamed Cossack and is now a ghost town, with but two or three stone buildings standing.

A map of the coast of northwest Australia from the original 1876 manuscript. The "NB" explains that the points on the map marked with letters are points of importance referred to in the script and identified by these letters

A typical Dalmatian barque of the 1870s, 775 tons, 150 feet overall length, slightly smaller than the Stefano

Point Maud area, about twenty-five miles south of Point Cloates, a full three days' march for the castaways. It was at the end of the third day that Deputy Captain Costa almost gave up the walk south because the soft sand and earthen pathways turned to sharp, rocky land underfoot (Point C)

Bay of Rest (Point V)

Termite mound, not a nest of "honeybees"

Bundegi Well, near Point S. The first evidence of white men's presence

The crested pigeon or topknot pigeon (Ocyphaps lophotes), described by Baccich in 1876 on his visit to Muiron Island (Point Z)

The cutter Jessie *at the rescue at Bundegi. The inscription at the base of the votive painting reads: "A solemn promise to Our Lady of Mercy was made by the two surviving seamen, Miho Baccich from Dubrovnik and Ivan Jurich from Pelješac, of the crew of the barque* Stefano, *under the command of the*

Captain Vlaho Miloslavich, which was shipwrecked in 1875 near Point Cloates in Australia. After six months of terrible sufferings, they were miraculously saved on April 18, 1876, by the English cutter Jessie *under the command of Captain Charles Tuckey"*

The author with Monica Vincent, granddaughter of Captain Vincent, Fremantle, 1987

Labels from Tuckey's canning factory in Mandurah

possibility of agonizing disappointment because of our hope that this could be our deliverance.

I'm sure everyone sensed our excitement as the small boat headed directly for shore. The women, especially, broke out in joyous shouts, encircling us and showering us with caresses amid frantic dancing. This must surely be a rescuer, at long last. We were ready to join in the joy at any moment. But once again it was not to be. The boat hove to only fifty feet away and we could easily see it was quite small, about twenty-five feet overall. It was loaded with people, all natives, not a white man among them. Two or three of the blacks wore clothes—shirts and trousers—a sure sign of closer contact with the world we were seeking to rejoin.

The natives were from a third tribe whose territory was east of Exmouth Gulf. They had journeyed here to another common meeting ground [Bay of Rest—Point V], having brought with them a large quantity of food, some tobacco, and some European clothing. The tribe landed and put their gear with the goods of the other two tribes. It was easy to see from the merriment that another feast was in the making.

I couldn't get interested in a celebration because of my disappointment over another "false rescue" and the long list of questions on my mind which were not only unanswered but also unasked. This new tribe must certainly have had close and recent contact with white men. The boat, the clothes, and many other little clues all begged to be explained. But there was no opportunity to talk with the new people. I had to be satisfied with an invitation to take a boat trip with them the next morning to an island [Point Z] slightly northeast of the Cape. My closest friend, Gjaki, would be with me, together with four others from the north and south tribes—Tondogoro, Tairo, Michi, and Naman—and ten men from the new tribe.

In retrospect, the trip proved to be foolhardy, but the novelty of such a venture was too attractive to ignore. We started at dawn from the Bay of Rest, intending to cover about forty miles to reach the island north of us. The official name of the island was Muiron, but the natives merely called it "island," no doubt after the English word they must have heard. The wind was in our teeth the entire way and what should have been a six-hour sail took all day. As we approached the island shortly before sunset,

I could see there were no harbors or bays along the eastern shore. The reef was three hundred feet or less from the beach, and as we sailed along it, looking for a safe passage to the shore, all but one of the natives jumped overboard and swam ashore, leaving Jurich and me with the helmsman, who was a cripple. My first reaction of fear was dispelled because I had learned not to under-estimate the wisdom of these people. Invariably, they knew what they were doing, and they had probably been here before. Less than a mile along the shore, we found a small passage through the reef and were able to beach the craft, secure it, and rush back to meet the others.

How glad I was that I had been invited, and I was even happier that I had come along in spite of my misgivings. The island was like another world. I wondered how it could be so different from the peninsula. There was no sandy desert, no barren plain—just lots of cool, green grass, thick bushes, and vegetation all the way from the hilltops to the water. What wonderful sounds came from the distant bushes. It was the song of thousands of beautiful birds only rarely seen on the mainland. It reminded me both sadly and joyously of my own home on the Adriatic.

The island was a small place, about seven miles long and two miles wide, mostly low land with a few rolling hills in the center. The climate differed from that on the mainland. The air was much cooler and damper. In fact, the night proved to be uncomfortably chilly, and a thick dew covered the whole island at dawn the next day.

There was time before dark to begin our search for the abundant food that was the principal reason for the trip. Turtle eggs were so plentiful and easy to find that we had gathered hundreds and could then turn our efforts to the special treat, the wild pigeons. They were quite beautiful, their heads crested by large tufts of jet-black feathers and the wings striped black and gold and tipped with white at the very edge. The upper neck was a mixture of warm bright colors, the breast was a dusty shade, and the eyes were bright pink.* The hunt was postponed until the next day, so we had a light supper of turtle eggs and retired early. The next

* A very accurate description of the crested pigeon (*Ocyphaps lophotes*), which over the ensuing century or so has adapted itself quite well to some of the urban areas of Australia.

morning, Jurich, the crippled man, and I were to stay at the campfire and keep it going while the others went after pigeons, pigeon eggs, and, of course, turtles. I regretted not being included because I wanted to see the natives' skill at capturing these elusive birds.

Early in the day the hunters returned loaded down with an amazing quantity and variety of birds as well as lots of fish, turtles, and eggs. Apparently the remoteness of the island and the rare appearance of the natives made the game easy prey. It was the sailboat which had abruptly changed all this, and I wondered how soon Muiron Island would be like the mainland, where the natives had to work so hard to catch or gather food.

Some of the men could not wait until we returned to the mainland but began to roast a few of their rarer delicacies. Others hauled their booty toward the boat, and a few men climbed the highest hill to light a bonfire to signal the tribes on the mainland of our success and impending return. Jurich and I were able to bring the boat to the spot where the men first scrambled ashore, and in no time at all, it was loaded beyond what was sensible for the boat's capacity. This was the first time I saw any waste; fifteen turtles and some eggs and birds had to be left on the beach. This upset me because I realized the introduction of the sailboat into the lives of these people had obviously brought with it some new evil they were not prepared to deal with. On the mainland not a single morsel of food had ever been gathered to excess.

The trip back was much shorter, only nine or ten miles to the nearest point on the peninsula, near the North West Cape [Point T], where Jurich had first reached the eastern shore. It was fortunate for us because the sea was very choppy and the wind quite strong, and it quickly got worse. The inexperience of the blacks added to our peril. The frail craft heeled over perilously close to its limit. The natives had no thought, or perhaps no knowledge, of shortening sail. Jurich and I were able to keep the sails appropriately trimmed to avoid jibing or capsizing. We arrived soon after sunset and could see a mob of people on the beach awaiting our arrival. It appeared that all three tribes had heeded our fire signal and had marched north to the end of the cape. The whole group numbered about one hundred and sixty, including those of us on the boat. This was the largest gathering I had yet seen.

As we approached the beach, many were walking into the water to intercept us. The boat was rushing to shore too fast and was out of control because the wind had risen abruptly. I feared that some injury to the people in the water was inevitable. But the helmsman abruptly veered about forty yards down shore and adroitly came up into the wind to beach the boat gently with no harm to people, cargo, or craft. It did not take long to unload the boat. No sooner had we sailors stepped ashore than the women rushed to us with a supply of cool, fresh water. There had been no water at all on the island and we had carried very little with us. The water was enough for Jurich and me; we settled down to sleep as the festivities began. The three tribes began feasting on the island delicacies. The wild orgy continued into the night until the constantly rising wind became a squall intense enough to put an end to the celebration. There was an unfortunate accident during the night. The boat was torn loose from its inadequate moorings and dashed against the rocks. A large hole near the keel caused the craft to sink. The natives begged Jurich to fix the boat because it had become indispensable for their coastal travel. But it was impossible; there were no suitable materials or tools to undertake such a demanding task. Jurich had to hide to avoid the appearance of being unwilling to help the natives.

8

Rescue

The morning after the violent squall, April 17, before the natives discovered their wrecked boat, Jurich woke me. "Wake up, Miho!" he cried excitedly. "Wake up! I had a wonderful dream last night. Today we will be saved!"

I responded sarcastically to the one who had, up to this moment, been so skeptical and negative. "So you believe in dreams now? Tell me all about it."

"I dreamed that a strong, stern Englishman came to this shore and took us on his boat to civilization."

"How stupid!" I said. "Don't you know that we dream what we wish to happen, especially if our wishes are impossible ones? What you have dreamed will not happen."

"You are so right," he sobbed and burst into tears. I, too, cried while wondering where my pretentious words of wisdom came from. But there was little time for self-pity because our part of the tribe was moving south a few miles, to the well at Bundegi, where I had first crossed to the east coast. We were prepared to stay there all day and, perhaps, the night. When we arrived, the daily search for food began, each person undertaking his task without direction or guidance. The old man Bengo, who usually spent all of his time weaving fishnets, broke the quiet with a loud voice. *"Tanic-balla Cialli komin!"* (Ship fellow Cialli coming!)

Three times in the past three weeks my hopes had been raised, followed by a severe letdown when hopes proved unfounded. Yet we were helpless to resist our longing for rescue. So, once again feeling like a fool, I rushed to the shore to see what Bengo was yelling about and, to my astonishment, saw a trim sloop, its bow facing the shore, less than a mile away. It was gleaming white and sparkled as it gently rose and fell on the bright blue water. The boat was rigged as a cutter, the kind often used as pilot boats because of their maneuverability. A single mast was stepped almost amidship with a long bowsprit to carry several headsails. I could see that the beam was narrow; the craft probably had a deep draft.

My mind began to whirl with a quick succession of thoughts —civilization, home, food I was accustomed to eat, clothes, family! I quickly recovered my composure and sent one of the men to find Jurich, who was off fishing with a small group. Then I climbed the nearest hill to see if I could attract the attention of the boat's crew.

The natives were assuring me that the vessel would definitely stop and that "Minara Cialli gogoj nulla!" (Shortly Cialli will come right here!)

Experience had taught me not to believe all their words of comfort, even though well intentioned, so I kept my eye on the vessel without relaxing. Slowly, but definitely, the bow swung away from land and the vessel began to move farther from shore. The anguish I felt is still easily recalled.

"Minara gogoj" (It will return shortly), my nearest friend said firmly.

"Mira gogoj" (It will not return), I replied, scowling.

By now Jurich had joined me, and the two of us angrily fired questions at the natives as if we knew that somehow they were conspiring to have us suffer disappointment once again. It was easy to be irrational in such an emotional situation. And how calm and positive was their reply. They said the ship never failed to stop. "Vac-balla gudara, bulac-balla gudara, sandi tobi nulla kughi cinaman." (There will be on board two white men, two natives, and a Chinese cook.) I interpreted this detailed account to mean that the ship belonged to two natives who had two whites with them, probably poor castaways like ourselves.

Meanwhile, the cutter had taken two tacks upwind and had now come about on a broad reach toward a passage in the Bundegi reef. In a moment the craft hove to and anchored, with sails still up but slack. I was bursting with excitement when I saw that a small dinghy was being launched astern.

As the dinghy came toward the beach, I still could not accept what the natives had taken for granted. Jurich joined me and we rushed into the water shouting wildly, I waving my tattered hat and he his cap. My friend Gjaki was by my side, and he puzzled me by saying that when Cialli got ashore, he would take Jurich and me with him to Tien Tsin or Pulimandur, together with Tondogoro and Cincigo, two carefully chosen men of the second tribe of the north. The water was perfectly calm as the little craft touched the beach. Just as the natives had said, there were two white men and two blacks. The two whites, probably apprehensive about this huge crowd of natives with two half-starved, sunburned whites in their midst, had drawn their revolvers so they could protect themselves if necessary.

As they stepped ashore, our amazement became theirs as soon as they studied the strange apparition of two gaunt boys, with patches of brown and pink skin and disheveled hair that had gone uncut for more than six months. I was clad only in shredded remnants of what had once been drawers, and I was holding an enormous floppy felt hat, a present from one of the recently arrived natives. Jurich was hardly better off, with the tatters of half a shirt over his shoulders and in his hand a ludicrously inappropriate sailor's cap, a relic from the *Stefano*.

We trembled as we exchanged stares with the two men. The older one approached us with his hand outstretched and a compassionate, or perhaps bewildered, look on his face. He spoke a few quiet words in English.

"No speak English," I muttered, half crying. Tears flowed as we shook hands, and joy filled my young heart as never before. Happiness was evident everywhere. The faces of our native friends were a sea of smiles as they shared this wonderful moment. The Englishman was so moved that he was also unable to hold back the tears. In a moment of reverie, a Latin phrase of thanksgiving from the beginning of the Holy Mass, a phrase I had often recited as an altar boy, sprang into my mind: *"Introibo ad altare Dei. Ad Deum qui laetificat juventutem meam!"* (I will go unto the altar of God. To God who giveth joy to my youth!)

The captain was quick to take charge. When he spoke, everyone, natives and crew, listened and responded. His first command was to get the two of us to the ship at once. His mate and the two black crewmen unloaded sacks of sugar for the natives, then took us to the cutter while the captain remained onshore with the tribes. The captain sent orders to the cook not to feed us anything but small amounts of bread and water because our stomachs would have to become accustomed to the new food very gradually.

Even the short trip from the shore to the boat was an emotional shock. As we pushed off from shore, I realized that in my haste and the overwhelming excitement I had not said a word of thanks to our black saviors—no goodbyes—no embraces, no tears—and there in the water, a few yards from the mob, stood my black brother Gjaki staring at us dolefully. I wanted to jump from the boat and rush back to embrace him, but I dared not. Civilized behavior did not permit this, and I was afraid to offend my rescuers. Thus I put out of my mind, and hoped to put out of my heart, the loving ties I had to the most gentle, loving friend I had known during my short life. It was more than a mere lad could handle. My state of mind and feelings were further confused by an ugly thought that popped into my head. Because I had been such a child of misfortune this past half year, perhaps this was another catastrophe. Perhaps this was a pirate ship and the captain was a slave merchant! Perhaps it was not too late to rush back to the black friends I knew and trusted.

At that moment the dinghy nudged into the hull of the moored ship and there on the quarterboard in letters of bright gold was the ship's name, *Jessie, Fremantle, W.A.* Suddenly the truth of our good fortune was solidly before us.

The welcome we had had from the captain and mate was exceeded by that of the Chinese cook, who pretended to obey the captain's diet orders. But no sooner had the mate and crew returned ashore than the cook put an immense bowl of rice and a platter of fried fish fillets before us. Needless to say, we devoured the whole fare quickly.

Ashore, a commotion occurred while the captain, mate, and crew were distributing the flour and sugar. The natives were beginning to quarrel and fight over items which they had never seen before. They could not bear to be deprived of them for even a moment. The captain left the shore because he felt he could not pacify such a large crowd consisting of three different tribes. We heard two pistol shots fired when he was halfway from the shore to the ship and later learned the shots were fired only in hopes of bringing the quarreling groups to their senses. When the dinghy pulled alongside, we were on deck to greet our benefactor. With him were Tondogoro and Cincigo, whom the natives had told me earlier would be leaving with Cialli. We were to learn more about this a bit later.

Soon after boarding, the captain weighed anchor and left the Exmouth Gulf, heading northeast toward Tien Tsin, the port on the northern coast of Australia, which the *Jessie* had left just a few days before. Below decks, as I rested in the warmth of the main cabin, my thoughts were all about the captain. Just who was he? For certain he was Cialli, the one whom the natives constantly prophesied would be our savior. We would soon get to know him as a strong man whose rough but handsome exterior so aptly reflected his adventurous life along the far-flung coast of his country. He was bronzed by the constant sun and strengthened by the hard ways of a pearl fisherman's life. But these were only surface characteristics of a person whose real strength and beauty resided in his character and personality. From the first moment of our meeting, it was easy to see that he was generous to a fault, and before long we saw one occasion after another when he was his brother's keeper—black and white brothers alike. I learned later that he had been born in Mandurah, near Fremantle. His forebears were from England. In recent years, pearl fishing had been his occupation, and he was well known and revered by the wandering tribes of the northwest coast. He always employed natives as divers and rotated them so the maximum number could learn. It was his practice to take with him on every trip to the pearling grounds two men from the local tribes. He first took them to Fremantle, where they lived, worked, and learned for a while. When he returned them to their tribes, their experience and increased understanding would, he hoped, benefit them in the face of new ways of life that were quickly surrounding them. The tribesmen, in some democratic way not known to me, selected their "ambassadors" well in advance of Tuckey's predictable arrival. I now understood how the natives could "forecast" that Tondogoro and Cincigo would be going to Fremantle with Jurich and me. Mistreatment of native pearlers, Malay as well as Australian, was legendary at that time. But, judging by the sincere, paternal approach of Charles Tuckey to his needy charges, I would

Captain Charles Tuckey, aged about thirty. The photo was given by Tuckey to young Baccich, who treasured it for the rest of his life

have to say the reports of mistreatment must have been exaggerated. His concern was evident in the presence of the two tribesmen he had just taken on board.

Another characteristic of this good man was his uncontrived humility. As often as we voiced our gratitude for what he had done and was still doing for us, he always replied that it was he who should be grateful to us for giving him the opportunity to do something so worthwhile.

More than once he reminded us how curiously fateful his finding us had been, suggesting that it was predestined. We learned that it was his boat, the *Jessie*, that I had sighted on the morning of April 12, five days before our rescue. He had no plans to stop at Exmouth Gulf this trip but was running non-stop from Tien Tsin to Fremantle when I saw his small cutter cross the north end of the gulf and disappear around the cape into the Indian Ocean. The same storm that hit the tribe after we left Muiron Island had already struck the *Jessie* and caused the captain to return to Exmouth Gulf for overnight refuge the night of April 16. The morning of the seventeenth they took the dinghy ashore to give their excess provisions to the tribes and discovered us.[†]

The next morning was beautiful, even though neither Jurich nor I had slept well because of the previous day's excitement (and some indigestion brought on by the cook's generosity). Tuckey, too, had trouble resting. When he checked on us during the night and noted our plight, he wisely had us move from the comfort of the sheltered cabin to the hard decks above, with the starry sky as our cover. We were soon fast asleep.

The first rays of sun the next morning were accompanied by a cry from the helm, "Sail ahead!" Captain Tuckey rushed above and saw a two-masted schooner heading for Fremantle from Tien Tsin. Tuckey, wanting to send a message ahead about our rescue,

---

[†] Another firsthand account of the rescue is recorded in the Memoirs of Hamlet Cornish (held in manuscript in the State Archives, Perth) and was published, with some strange aberrations, in *The West Australian,* June 12, 1979. However, it adds very little to the story. Aged twenty-one at the time, Cornish had family connections with Tuckey and was serving as first mate aboard the *Jessie* on his first trip north. He gives a good description of pearling operations and says they had had a profitable season; they employed twenty-five natives as divers, and had subsequently returned them to their home territory along the coast. A few years later, Cornish was a pioneer of the pastoral industry in the Kimberley district.

invited the captain of the schooner to board us. The visitor offered to lend an extra crew member to eliminate the need to return to Tien Tsin to take on extra help. With four new passengers on board, this was necessary. Tuckey eagerly accepted the offer, but he declined to accept the other offer for one or both of us survivors to sail back on the schooner so the new captain might learn of our adventures and further reduce Tuckey's burden. Tuckey replied, "No, no, my friend. It is better not to separate them, as they may need each other's company for a while longer. They have suffered through so much together."

There was an exchange of provisions, and both ships steered for Fremantle, the schooner outpacing us considerably. We stopped for the night at anchorage off an uninhabited island west of the Dampier Archipelago. We went ashore only to gather firewood for the cook. At dawn the following morning we left.

Nine days went by without a stop as we once again rounded the North West Cape and headed south along the coast, barely out of sight of land. In the Point Cloates area, almost at the spot where the *Stefano* broke up, we met an Australian barque, the *Alexandra*, heading in the opposite direction to Tien Tsin. The story of the *Stefano* and the presence of the survivors had been made known to the *Alexandra* with the request that this information be reported in Tien Tsin. As it developed, the message was not clearly understood at the pearling port, causing the government vessel *Victoria* to be fitted out immediately to go on a search for survivors.

The expedition under Captain Walcott stopped at Exmouth Gulf first, and the natives explained that only two had survived and had already been rescued. Nevertheless, the *Victoria*, taking a native tribesman on board, sailed around the coast to Point Cloates, where they visited the original campsite near Camp Hill [Point B]. From their reports, everything was just as we had left it, and of course they found no more survivors. The *Victoria* returned the native to his tribe and continued back to Tien Tsin.

Our journey down the coast was restful and happy. I was spending most of my time getting to know and understand Tondogoro and Cincigo. The cook had relieved them of the large amount of turtle meat they brought on board and was introducing them to food that was new and strange to them. Tondogoro was still noticeably uneasy. He had wept uncontrollably as he left his people and looked at every new experience with wide-eyed amazement. Cincigo was more sophisticated, or pretended to be. He laughed at his partner's mistakes, teased him when he became alarmed, and constantly offered advice. I thought to myself: if they only knew what was yet in store for them!

On the ninth day at sea we entered Shark Bay, a large harbor-like indentation south of the Gascoyne River. Tuckey had by now told us that our party of ten survivors would not have found a settlement at the mouth of the Gascoyne. At least, he had never heard of any, although an occasional pearling vessel might shelter briefly in the small estuary there. A better objective for a possible rescue would have been at the mouth of the Ashburton River, north and east of the shipwreck, about two hundred miles away. Tuckey also said most of the natives we had met would have known this. Once in Shark Bay, we anchored by Dirk Hartog Island, most of which was owned by a colonist who had established a large sheep station there.‡

Captain Tuckey was an old acquaintance of the family but had not seen them in the past ten years, so he was understandably excited when we went ashore. He brought us, Jurich and me, with him, plus the mate and the two tribesmen. The Englishman and his family seemed delighted to see the captain after such a long absence and were quite excited about meeting his unusual guests. Jurich and I, together with our native companions, were put in the care of the two young children of the family. They took us through the entire home and around the grounds, giving us an opportunity to explain to Tondogoro and Cincigo in their own language every little detail of whatever was new or strange to them. This must have been an exciting day for them. For me, it was a day of contentment because I was again back in civilization. Following lunch, we spent some time playing English parlor games, then left the family and the island at dusk.

A minor incident interrupted our journey. We ran aground on a sandbar while trying to take a shorter route around the south

---

‡ F. L. Von Bibra was the holder of the grazing rights on the island, and he, too, had been engaged in shipping activities and pearling.

end of the island. Captain Tuckey, always cool and controlled, sent everyone off to sleep to await the high tide, which he knew would occur in about eight hours. It came in on schedule, and with fine winds and good weather we entered the harbor of Fremantle on May 5, 1876—Pulimandur at last!

9

Fremantle

Fremantle was a small town, about 32° south, at the mouth of the Swan River. The population was about 2,500, and the town proper had about four hundred houses arranged in the typically English geometric pattern of north–south, east–west grids. At the south end was a long jetty with a large navigation light to help ships avoid submerged rocks. A lighthouse was near the mouth of the river, and another one was twelve miles away on Rottnest Island. The harbor was very well defined.

The story of our shipwreck and rescue had preceded us, and there was a large crowd at the docks waiting for us to tie up. Poor Tondogoro could not handle the excitement—so many boats, hundreds of houses, and, most of all, so many whites. *"Suogaja ciullu vac-balla!"* (What a large crowd of whites!)

He was quite frightened when a number of them boarded the *Jessie*, so he hid in the cargo hold and peered at the visitors through the cracks. The harbor master and the chief of police were among the first to visit. Later a businessman whose birthplace was Rovinj came to offer his services as an interpreter. How nice it was to hear the Italian tongue once again!

After the formalities, Captain Tuckey went ashore with Jurich, the two visiting natives, and me. The natives had managed to get into some ill-fitting clothes. The captain gave me some money to buy fresh fruit for them because they had not eaten much of the strange food aboard ship. Then he left us for a short while. Later

Fremantle jetty, ca. 1870, with Customs shed on the left

we went to the Customs House to take care of some other formalities. The harbor master, who had come aboard the *Jessie* earlier, had one of his men take Jurich and me to a nearby store where he bought us each a pair of shoes and some stockings to replace the makeshift items lent to us by the men on the *Jessie*. When we returned to the Customs House, there was a bit of commotion. A rather loud, excited individual, hurried and out of breath, had rushed to the hall where we were being interviewed and offered to take charge of us and assume all responsibility. He was short and stout, with a full beard and an air of great confidence.

He kept repeating to all in hearing distance that he was, like us, originally from the Dubrovnik area. He had been born nearby, on the small island of Šipan. He overwhelmed us with warm affection and was genuine in his delight at seeing two fellow countrymen for the first time in the seventeen years since he had left the Dalmatian coast. He delighted in speaking incessantly with us in Croatian and in Italian, much to the amusement of the Customs House officials. With Captain Tuckey's permission, he took us back to the clothing store, where he outfitted us from head to toe while he gave us a detailed story of his life.

Vicko Vukovich was his name, but he was known here as Captain Vincent. He was owner or master of a coastal schooner and ran his own small trading business. After fitting us out to his satisfaction, he insisted on taking us home to meet his wife, a generous, happy Irishwoman from Limerick, and his five children. Captain Vincent's next undertaking was to busy himself sending cablegrams to our families. He said a recent cable link between India and Istanbul now enabled direct communication, in only a few days, from Perth to Rijeka, the home port of the once beautiful *Stefano*.

When Vincent returned us to the Customs House, Captain Tuckey greeted us with a generous offer of employment. His first mate had decided to remain ashore, and Tuckey felt our training, experience, and knowledge of the Aborigines' language would suit us well for the pearling trade. This man's goodness toward us knew no limit! As generous as this offer was, we had to confess our longing to return home to our families. However, I had the pleasure of spending a few days at the home of Captain Tuckey and his parents at Mandurah, a tiny village about forty miles farther south along the coast.

There were other interesting developments in the next two weeks, and even the governor of the colony came down from Perth to meet us. On May 8 the authorities held a preliminary inquiry into the wreck of the *Stefano* at the Customs House, and we survivors gave our evidence, with Vincent serving as interpreter. We were told that a report would be sent to the Board of Trade in London for further communication to Rijeka. The government in Perth also decided that the Aborigines who had succored us should be sought out and rewarded, but should be made to understand that the reward would have been even greater had they saved our whole party. It was said that, in four or five days of walking, they could have got a vessel sent out from Tien Tsin to rescue us all. Arrangements were made for Captain Vincent to take the government's gifts to the natives on his next voyage north, which was imminent. I eagerly offered to take part in such an expedition so as to add my own appreciation to the official reward.

Meanwhile, feeling that the cable service might be unreliable, I carefully compiled and mailed a written letter to my parents, assuring them that I was still alive and well:

Fremantle, Western Australia
May 16, 1876

Dear Parents,

I'm sure that you, as well as the others that know me, think of me as a dead man, and believe me, I wasn't too far from that. Now I'll tell you about the terrible tragedy which occurred from October 27, 1875, until April 18, 1876.

Last year on October 27 at 2 a.m., the barque *Stefano* under the command of Captain Vlaho Miloslavich was wrecked on a reef near the North West Cape of Australia. As soon as the barque struck, it heeled over to the right side and in less than three hours the ship broke up completely into large and small wreckage. We did everything possible to launch the lifeboats, but it was all in vain because the sea was so rough. At the captain's order, a small dinghy was lowered over the stern and the captain, lieutenant, one seaman, and I got aboard. But what happened then? The moment the boat touched the sea, it overturned. I was lucky to grab the keel; the others I never saw again. Thus, frightened, in the dark night, I floated for ten hours. Finally I succeeded in getting ashore where, almost half-dead, I threw myself on the bare, hot sand, hoping to see some of my companions. Soon I was able to see Karlo Costa floating on the ship's ladder, then the boatswain and other sailors came floating on various parts of the wrecked ship. Ten of us were saved. All, half-dead, stretched out near me; we stayed there, naked, all the day, unable to walk because our feet were becoming swollen. The next day we decided to search for food and drink and we found various kinds of it floating up to us from the ship. We decided to build a hut out of the pieces broken off from the shipwreck. Next morning we saw some naked savages, men and women. At first we were frightened that they were cannibals, but they didn't do us any harm.

Finally we went in search of a river which was only a few miles ahead, as the officer had told us. We walked for six days, and if we hadn't met some savages who helped us by showing us a water well, we would all have died of thirst in the middle of all that sand. We stayed by the water for three days and then we moved on because we were told we were only two miles distant from the river. We went on foot for three days but we didn't find any water, so we turned back. We lived for three months eating only raw shellfish and having no fire to cook with. We drank plain water. You should know that we lost all our strength during that period and looked like skeletons; we were dying quickly. It stormed at Christmas and it lasted for three days. During that time we didn't have any food, as we couldn't find anything to eat. Two men died at that time, and after a few days six more also died. My companion and I survived, probably because we had more strength. But later we, too, nearly died of hunger. When the black savages came again, we clasped our hands, begging them to give us something to eat. They were deeply concerned and took us with them and gave us some fish to eat and some water to drink. We stayed with them for three months, totally naked, looking for food almost all the time. We saw several ships passing by, but they couldn't see us.

At last, on April 18, 1876, an English cutter came near the coast. The photo, enclosed in this letter, shows the captain of this ship, Captain Charles Tuckey, who saved our lives. We sailed for seventeen days with them until we came to the port of Fremantle, which has about six hundred inhabitants.

The English, hearing about our terrible accident, took us ashore and gave us food and money. In this small port, we found a rich gentleman from the island of Šipan, who has been here for seventeen years. He is married and has five children. His present name is Mr. Vincent, but his real name is Vicko Vukovich. He gave us some clothes and some money, too. We are staying at his place now. His wife is treating us like her own children. He owns several ships. Soon we will embark on a schooner under his command for five liras per month.

He is sending two letters to his relatives because he hasn't heard anything about them and I beg you to inquire and let me know whether there are some of his relatives still alive so that he could help them.

The Englishman, the master of the cutter, after having questioned me about navigation, praised me in front of many fine gentlemen and asked if I would join his ship as an officer. I thanked him and told him I had already been assigned to a ship owned by my family, but I promised to visit him on my way back to Fremantle (which

Captain Vincent and his family, about 1875. Left to right: John, Mrs. Vincent (Bridget Russel), Mary, Andrew, Captain Vincent, and Joan

will be in exactly two months' time). He agreed and stated in front of all those gentlemen that he himself will pay for my officer's exam. Noticing his kindness, I asked him teasingly why he favored me so. He replied, "First of all, you're very professional, and you're not like the local seamen, who are always drunk, which I really don't like."

I now speak English very well. It was said here that the natives had been nourishing us so that they could eat us. All the citizens here are anxious to meet us, so they keep on inviting us for lunch or dinner. They have taken a lot of photos of us and everyone wants one. I'm sending you one which is not the best of my photos because my eyes are still hurting me. I'll also send you the photo of our countryman and his wife as well as the photo of all the survived crew of the *Stefano*, which is me and my friend Jurich from Pelješac.

I hope you're happy to know your son loves you and will never forget you.

You'll get my letters every four weeks because I can mail them only once a month. People here collected twenty pounds to help us. On the twenty-first of this month there will be a drama performed showing the terrible tragedy which occurred on the night of October 27, 1875. The money collected from selling the tickets will also be given to us. As soon as we get it I'll let you know the exact sum. I'll write to my Uncle Nikola today so that he, too, gets some news of me. Write to me whether the number of my brothers and sisters has increased.

We are immensely happy and very grateful for being saved, especially since the natives have previously eaten several persons. We could have died as well. The two of us were the first ones that have escaped from the natives' hands. I have so many things to write to you, but it's enough for today. I'll write to you more about me in my next letter.

Give my regards to Uncle Ivan and his family as well as to all the others who thought me dead. Give my regards to Kate; has she gone to the nunnery yet? I've no space to write you more. Goodbye,

Yours faithfully,
Miho Baccich*

---

* The original of this letter is in the Maritime Museum in Dubrovnik.

Miho Baccich and Ivan Jurich shortly after their rescue, Fremantle, 1876

And so it was that I said farewell to Charles Tuckey and the two natives from "my tribe" and on May 27 boarded Captain Vincent's schooner, the *Rosette*. I made my farewell brief and, as best I could, unemotional because I knew it would take so little for me to break down as I had so often done in the past month. Besides, I hoped I would see everyone again when I returned to Fremantle, although we all knew this was unlikely.

The trip to Tien Tsin was uneventful and quick—just eight days. But to my regret we stayed there nearly a month while Vincent completed his business. Also, because the schooner *Victoria*, which had been sent to search for additional survivors, had not been heard from for some time, there were fears for its safety. Vincent felt it appropriate to wait a while longer for its return.

We found Tien Tsin to be a small town nestling on a small hill gently sloping toward a little bay. It had only three houses of stone; the others were of wooden frame with thatched roofs. There were about three hundred whites; the rest were all natives. All around the town were grassy plains, drained by a small, clear stream that emptied into the bay. At low tide the ships rested on the dry seabed. The main commerce of the town was the exportation of copper from nearby mines.

On June 28, the *Victoria* sailed into port. We were among the first to board her and were astonished to see that the ship had brought back all of the relics left behind at the original campsite, reminders of such sorrowful days. Prominent among them was the cabin door of the *Stefano* upon which poor Costa had carved the ship's name, the date, and the names of the crew. We also learned that a lot of other big wreckage had been found along the same stretch of beach, some of it clearly from much older ships. Apparently, the cruel cyclone at Christmastime had dislodged further material that had been wedged against the reefs for many long years.

Two days later we left for Fremantle with plans to cruise the Exmouth Gulf in search of the tribes who were to receive our gifts. We met with quick success. On July 4, at Vlamingh Head, the western extremity of the North West Cape, we came upon the tribes we had left eleven weeks before. Their numbers had increased; apparently a fourth tribe had joined them.

As the launch approached the shore, the natives ran off, probably because there was such a crowd of us in the small boat—

Captain Vincent and Walcott, the captain of the *Victoria*, who was now traveling with us, several passengers from Tien Tsin, Jurich, and I. As we got closer to shore, I knew we had found the right group because I recognized several of the stragglers whose curiosity prompted them to stay in the open. I signaled wildly with my hat, and my old friends recognized me. The news was passed on to the others, who came down to the water in hordes to greet us. Several jumped in the water and pulled the boat up on the beach. How wonderful and amazing to see these good people again and to witness their happiness in seeing us—their old friends. We were showered with the familiar pats and hugs and the women circled Jurich and me and danced joyfully.

All this enthusiasm was overshadowed by their reaction to the gifts we unloaded and distributed—sugar, flour, tobacco, tools, and many other items. Such loud screaming and jostling to get the good objects! To my great joy and relief, I found Gjaki in the midst of them and had an opportunity to make amends for my seeming indifference when we parted soon after our rescue.

Gjaki was quite upset, but not about my abrupt departure. He made it very clear that it was inappropriate for me to bring gifts to the whole tribe, including some I had never met. Custom, it seems, dictated that he as my former provider and guardian should be the sole owner of all items. With quick thinking and some diplomacy, I explained to him that because I was no longer a member of the tribe, I must follow the rules of the people I was now living with, and those rules held me responsible for rewarding everyone. However, I added, I was free to give him a special gift. With that, I produced the leather belt with sheath knife which I had bought for him in Fremantle. His attitude changed as abruptly as the expression on his face. What a beautiful wide grin he wore as he strapped the belt and knife around his completely nude body!

The women had opened the sugar and were consuming it by pouring the sugar on the sand and then spreading themselves full length on the ground and licking it up with great gusto and much smacking of lips. The mirrors seemed to cause the most commotion because many natives had never seen their reflections before. The flour, which had before been highly treasured, remained untouched. It could not compete with all the novel items.

The next thing that drew their attention was the small firearm which Captain Walcott had brought along. "Give it to me," said one of the natives. And to the question of what he would do with it came a ready answer: *"Tungoro aggin nulla pignari cominini."* (I will shoot the quarrelsome women.) I am saddened to mention that Jurich's friend Gjimmi was not to be found in the group. He had left the cape area some time earlier with a smaller tribe.

This time I felt I expressed my gratitude and said a proper goodbye to these dear souls whom I loved so much, and there was no sadness as the natives shoved our skiff back into the sea. Everyone was happy and smiling—that is, until we got out of sight, when once again my tears returned. I may have matured more rapidly than normal in the previous six months, but it appeared I was still a crybaby at heart.

A week later we were back in Fremantle. This time I felt an overwhelming urge to hurry home. But it was not until three weeks later that passage home could be arranged. In the interim, we stayed with Captain Vincent. The colonial government put up the money for our fares, expecting reimbursement from Austria, and we were presented with ample pocket money for the voyage thanks to the public entertainments that had been held for our relief. The dramatic performance that we had originally expected to take part in before going north had been canceled when, a few days before, the good people of Fremantle suffered another tragedy close at hand; this was the wreck of the cutter *Gem* off Rottnest Island, with the loss of all ten men aboard. Instead, they had mounted a benefit concert on June 8, which was so successful that a second one was put on a week later.* Half the money so raised was given to Jurich and me, and half to the relatives of the men lost in the *Gem.*

---

* The chief promoter of these events was James Pearce, ex-convict, bookseller and stationer, and proprietor of Fremantle's vigorous weekly newspaper. These variety concerts, of the style then in vogue at both port and capital, embraced all kinds of vocal, instrumental, and literary offerings, along with the band of the Rifle Volunteers. At the second concert, Pearce made considerable exactions on the sympathies of all present with his vivid rendering of a maudlin poem entitled "The Ship That Went Down" by Adah Isaacs Menken, a celebrated actress who hailed from New Orleans. The Oddfellows' Hall was "crowded to suffocation" on the eighth, and the audience was again very numerous and fashionable on the sixteenth.

Baccich, left, and Jurich, right, probably posing for a scene in the proposed benefit performance of the shipwreck drama designed to raise money for the boys' trip home

And so on August 7, after saying goodbye to Captain Vincent and other kind people, we took the little coastal steamer *Georgette*[+] to the port of Albany on the south coast of Western Australia to await passage overseas. A week later, we boarded a British mail steamer bound for Galle in Ceylon, two weeks away. There we transferred to the steamer *Indus* en route from Japan, and continued to Aden, through the Red Sea, and on to Suez, another voyage of two weeks. At Suez the Austrian consul[‡] took charge of us and within two days had us on a train to Alexandria. From there an Austro-Hungarian steamer took us the final leg home, a trip of eight days, to Trieste at the head of the Adriatic. Rijeka, the home port of the poor *Stefano*, was about twenty-five miles away. By October 27, one year after our shipwreck, I was back again with my parents, my sisters and brothers, and many dear friends who had long mourned me for dead.

[+] The *Georgette*, too, came to grief four months later when again bound for Albany. Having sprung a bad leak, it had to be beached in the heavy surf near the mouth of the Margaret River. Several of its fifty-eight passengers drowned, and more would have been lost had it not been for the heroic efforts of a local settler's daughter, Grace Bussell, and a black stockman, Sam Isaacs. Having witnessed the scene from the coast, the pair repeatedly rode their horses into the surf and carried many people to safety before the ship sank.
[‡] From 1867 to 1918, Dalmatia and Croatia were under the dual monarchy of Austria-Hungary.

10

Home Again and a New World

Almost from the day of my arrival, I could see that my rehabilitation would not be easy. While I thoroughly enjoyed the attention and affection of my close family, there were other aspects of the homecoming that pained me. People in the streets stared rudely at me and made thoughtless remarks. Some neighbors thought nothing of pointing me out and commenting loudly about "the one who came back from the dead." "What happened to all of your shipmates?" "Did you see the cannibals?" I avoided going out and mixing with the crowds for weeks.

Another difficult situation arose. My father, in all propriety, expected me to call on all of the families of my former shipmates, at least those to whom I was related or with whom I had been friendly. He simply did not know how painful this would be for me. So many times I had to repeat the details of the tragedy, which were torture for me to recall. When I visited Bucich's mother in Rijeka, she wanted to know just how and where he was buried. I had to explain that he was one of the last two to die, and by then Jurich and I were simply not strong enough to bury our comrades. All the while my tortured conscience was reliving the disgraceful scene when we had attempted to save ourselves at the expense of her dead son!

But there were also some pleasant experiences. My father engaged a Jesuit scholar, Father Skurla, of Dubrovnik, to help me write a record of the shipwreck. Jurich and I met with Father

Skurla at the Jesuit rectory several times and told our story in detail. It was good to talk to someone who was so sympathetic and understanding. The record he made of our recollections was accurate, and Jurich and I both liked it. The original was for my father, and one copy was made for my Uncle Nikola, owner of the *Stefano*.*

However, the grisly experiences continued to mount up. I noticed a memorial plaque made of marble in my parish church. Some friend or relative had it placed near a large array of votive candles. It was in memory of me! A generous thought, I'm sure, but extremely unsettling to the one it commemorated.

My father quickly had the memorial replaced with another more appropriate commemoration. In thanksgiving for my survival, he commissioned the leading maritime artist of the Adriatic, Bozi Ivankovich, a retired sea captain, to paint a picture of the rescue scene with the cutter *Jessie*, from descriptions and crude sketches I furnished.*

To help me escape from the troubling atmosphere and also to further my education and career, my father sent me to the Royal Government Maritime Academy at Rijeka, where, in 1878, I completed my studies. My Uncle Nikola, who lived in Rijeka, had a new ship under construction to replace the *Stefano*. It was to be called the *Resurrection*. I rather liked that! My family decided I should attend the academy for an additional year in order to complete the requisites for my master's, or captain's, papers. In December 1879, the same month the *Resurrection* was launched, I received my captain's papers.

I was named captain of the new ship. I suppose I should have been very grateful. In fact, I was somewhat embarrassed and very concerned about whether I deserved it. I wondered if I would ever have the satisfaction and pride of being a self-made man like Charles Tuckey or Captain Vincent, who had got their ships by their hard work. It would have been excessively ungrateful to decline the captaincy. But from the day I boarded the ship, I was looking for an opportunity to leave.

* The original manuscript is now in the possession of the author. The handwritten duplicate copy is in the National Museum in Rijeka, Croatia, a gift from Danica Lenac Presic, Baccich's niece.
* This votive painting by the highly regarded maritime artist hangs in the rectory of the Church of Our Lady of Mercy in Dubrovnik.

The city of New Orleans and the Mississippi River, 1851. Lake Pontchartrain in the distance

Because a trip to the Orient was under consideration, I at first expected to have a chance to return to Western Australia and join the band of entrepreneurs who seemed so heroic and successful. I felt I would have my family's blessing, but the ship's destination was unexpectedly changed to America, and in due course I found myself there approaching its shores.

If I wanted to leave the ship, I would have to consider New Orleans as a place to do so. I knew there was a small group of Dalmatian settlers in the city because arrangements had been made for me to provision the ship at the store of a countryman, Andrew Cietcovich from Boka Kotorska. I wanted to leave the ship; both my instincts and my mind suggested I should. So I spent a sleepless night in the fog at the mouth of the Mississippi River downstream from the city, anxious to get to the port as soon as the morning fog lifted.

Toward dawn, the wind shifted out of the north and the temperature dropped. This cleared away most of the fog, and before long we were under way by tow. The city was not visible until we were right on it because it was located around a large bend on the east bank.

I couldn't have been more surprised when I went ashore. We

were able to moor alongside the French Market, a place where fresh food of all varieties was displayed in many open stalls. Cietcovich's store was across the street from the market. He met our ship and took me back to his store to discuss business and tell me about the city. On the short walk of some three hundred yards, I was amazed to hear Italian, Croatian, French, and English all being spoken in the market area. Cietcovich explained that there were sizable groups of settlers from many areas living in the original part of town, the Vieux Carré, or Old Quarter. Spanish, German, and Irish settlers were also present in large numbers. How ironic that in my first glimpse of America, where I expected to find Americans or men of English origin, I found a very European city with a variety of Europeans.

During the next week, I was to discover many attractive features of this exciting place. First, it was so large and dynamic—over 200,000 residents! The Croatian colony was also large, nearly a thousand people, and Cietcovich introduced me to many of them. A large number were already owners of their own small businesses, retail stores, restaurants, and oyster fisheries (a favorite business among Dalmatians). It was not only the air of prosperity in New Orleans that impressed me but also the cultural resources of such a unique place. There was an opera house in the old town only a few streets away. There was a university a few miles north, in the new area. Two old government buildings built by the Spanish were on a plaza just a short distance from the ship, one building on each side of a beautiful cathedral. The cathedral I believe had been built by the French (it was named for St. Louis). The climate was warm and pleasant, and the food and wine unbelievably fine and varied.

There were a considerable number of blacks in the town. I was interested and curious because of the desire to renew my friendships with the blacks who had saved my life in Australia. I learned from Cietcovich that whites did not fraternize with blacks in New Orleans, but that did not mean they mistreated them. He also pointed out that these blacks were Africans, perhaps implying that they were inferior to the Australian blacks. I learned that it wasn't even fifteen years since slavery had been abolished in the town. Even so, I thought it nice to be among blacks again, and I took advantage of every chance to talk to them and be friendly, but they were very shy and puzzled about my advances. Some looked so much like my brothers on the North West Cape that seeing them tugged hard at my emotions. Others were very different in every way, including color. Many looked like the North Africans and Egyptians we had encountered in Mediterranean ports on our way home from Australia.

I was fast convincing myself that New Orleans was where I wanted to be. But where and how would I start? One thing that I had noticed made it easier to make a decision. Cietcovich, when he met my ship, was the perfect picture of a store owner, with coat, starched shirt, necktie, and the bundle of official-looking papers that he was carrying. But at his store he worked in shirt sleeves and joined his small crew in nearly all tasks. At dockside, he dressed like the black dockhands and worked alongside them unloading and loading the ship. I liked his egalitarian approach to work. Maybe Cietcovich could help me get started.

For four days I had been socializing with the local Croatians, and I saw a camaraderie that I had never known before. My mind was made up! So after a dinner that I attended with Cietcovich, I boldly asked him if he would hire me to do whatever it was he needed done and said that I was not above doing any of the work that I had seen him do.

He had mixed reactions to my proposal. Although he was willing to help any countryman in need, he felt a sea captain with my education, experience, and family position was just not his idea of a man in need. However, when he learned that I had already determined that I must change my life, my goals, and my homeland, whether in America or in Australia, he modified his position.

"Very well," he said. "You can begin any moment you wish. You will have a room and a kitchen on the second floor of my store and that will be a third of your pay." I went to his home on Royal Street early the next morning to meet his wife, Nina, who was also from Boka Kotorska. I also met his only child, Angelina, who was about twelve years old and had been born in New Orleans. When I left their home, I walked directly to the *Resurrection* to pick up a small duffel bag of clothes, my chronometer, and my glass. As I walked up Royal Street toward the square, the Cathedral bells were ringing wildly in high pitch, and it suddenly dawned on me that it was November 1, the eve of the feast of All Souls, which celebrates the hoped-for resurrection of the dead!

EPILOGUE

If this tale were to end on the preceding page, there would be several important questions left unanswered. Perhaps the first question is one raised by several persons who read the story while it was being prepared for publication: Why would Miho Baccich appear to desert his ship, shipmates, family, and homeland so suddenly on his first ocean voyage as captain of the *Resurrection*?

The situation was not as it might appear. Interviews with Miho's descendants and a review of correspondence with his family in Dalmatia and Croatia reveal otherwise.

As was mentioned in the introduction, when the ships of iron with steam engines came into existence, the maritime nations and cities of the Adriatic—from Venice and the Istrian Peninsula southward to the Bay of Kotor—went into a rapid decline. Emigration from the Dalmatian coast was widespread in the middle to late 1800s.

Ports of entry around the world were inevitably the ports of call familiar to Dalmatian seamen, especially those locations which shared the mild climate of the Mediterranean: San Francisco and New Orleans; Buenos Aires; Sydney and Perth, Australia, and Auckland, New Zealand, were favorites. Sizable colonies of Dalmatians were already there by the mid-1800s.

Baccich's daughter (and my mother) Euxenia indicated that by the time he had completed his studies at the maritime academy, Miho had made up his mind to emigrate to Australia or America

Baccich in New Orleans, about 1882

at the earliest opportunity. Presumably his intentions were known to his uncle Nikola Baccich as the ship's owner, to his parents, and to the second-in-command of the *Resurrection*.

What happened to Jurich in the years following their adventure? In the account we are told only that Jurich was an ordinary seaman, eighteen years old, from a town called Oskorušno. We can conclude from the substance of the same manuscript that the relationship between Jurich and Baccich was for the most part close, although there had been episodes of conflict such as the fight following the death of Dediol, the last man who perished. Although the two young men had struggled bitterly for a full day until they collapsed on the sand, following their "adoption" by the Aboriginal tribe they were mutually supportive and friendly. The only conflict we see is Baccich's reprimand of Jurich for striking a woman in a fit of anger and despair a few days before their rescue. Their relationship must have seemed supportive to Captain Tuckey, who refused to separate them when a passing ship's captain wanted to assist Tuckey by caring for one of the lads. Tuckey felt their continuing companionship was necessary when once again in new surroundings.

All in all, it would seem that their being the only survivors would be the foundation of a lifelong friendship. It is, therefore, puzzling that Baccich corresponded with Captain Tuckey (though rather sparingly) for at least twenty-five years following the rescue, but there is no record of his keeping in touch with Jurich. Nor does he mention Jurich in his letters to Tuckey. We do know that they shared some time in Baccich's hometown of Dubrovnik shortly after their return from Australia. Father Stjepan Skurla acknowledges the participation of both in the preface of the manuscript he prepared: "Shortly after their rescue, Baccich and Jurich narrated all of the events set forth in this story while the facts were fresh in their minds."

My curiosity led me to try to locate Oskorušno, Jurich's hometown, and to learn whatever I could about his life after the young men returned. I had already determined to trace Baccich's other ancestors in Dubrovnik and on the island of Korčula. I pored over modern maps of the Dalmatian coast and the Adriatic without finding Oskorušno, which I thought might have been a name in use in the last century but now displaced by something very different. Many Dalmatian towns had borne Italian names during the height of the Republic of Venice. Dubrovnik was formerly known as Ragusa, Rijeka was called Fiume, and Mali Lošinj was called Lussinpiccolo. I also suspected the town was very small and perhaps not well known. Even my inquiries upon arriving at Rijeka brought no results.

I then shifted my attention to the island of Korčula, where I had some leads on Baccich's ancestors. My search for Jurich would have to wait until I could find a more systematic way to locate Oskorušno. I departed Rijeka by boat for an overnight trip to Korčula, about one hundred miles down the Adriatic coast. Before embarking, I bought detailed maritime charts so I could follow the coastline and island geography of the voyage. As the ship neared Korčula, I began to study closely the area on the charts. My interest centered on the adjacent narrow peninsula called Pelješac, which extends from the mainland some fifty miles north-west into the Adriatic until it nearly meets the island of Korčula. Quite by accident I noticed a tiny dot on the peninsula a short distance across the straits from Korčula—Oskorušno! I looked at the information included with the charts, but could find only a little about the village: population 161, and its distance about ten miles from the small town of Orebić.

When I left the ship, I hurried to catch a small ferry to Orebić, where I spent the night and prepared for a trip to Oskorušno the next morning. Luckily, I was able to reserve one of the three taxis in town. Because I knew that all but the most recent family records were kept in the churches and that parish priests were usually well informed on local genealogy, I planned to begin my search at the village church.

The priest lived adjacent to the church and spoke English. He was very interested in my story but was quick to let me know the bad news. First, all of the old parish records had been destroyed in the early 1940s when a sizable contingent of German soldiers landed at Korčula and the nearby port of Orebić. Shortly after their arrival, the Germans learned about the many fine vineyards in the highland valley around Oskorušno and set out to find some wine. The news traveled faster than the soldiers, so that when they arrived, there was no wine in the vats but plenty on the ground! Enraged by this, the Nazi invaders ransacked the church, piled all of the vestments and the records (some dating back to the fifteenth century) in the churchyard, doused them with gasoline, and set them on fire.

To add to this bad news, the young priest explained that his predecessor, who had known everyone for miles around, had recently died. He himself knew very little about the ancestry of his parishioners. My taxi driver listened attentively and showed not a little sadness at the failure of my search. He mentioned a very well educated relative of his wife who spoke English and might know something about Jurich. After traveling several miles off the main road, we came to a roadside sign which read "Ohranovići." Marko Ohranovich was not expected home until about noon. The driver said we shouldn't wait because he would have to leave the meter running, which would be expensive.

He drove very slowly as we left, almost as if lost. Suddenly he stopped, jumped out, and ran to the side of the road to shout at someone in a field. It was Marko, and the driver told him to come up to the road because an *Engleski* wanted to talk to him. Even from a distance, I could see that Marko was not young, and I thought I should go to meet him. The driver suggested we meet at the house. Marko, a tall, handsome man of about seventy years, greeted us and invited us into the main house, which had been built in the twelfth century and had housed the family for seven generations. His English was excellent, so I began telling the story of the shipwreck to explain my desire to learn about Jurich. I had barely begun when Ohranovich exclaimed, "Please wait a moment! The story is already well known to me and to all of the older people in this village. I want to tell you something of importance. One of our local boys, Ivan Jurich, was the co-survivor of the shipwreck with your grandfather!" I quickly told him the purpose of my visit was to learn what had happened to Jurich in the years following his return.

In an almost poetic manner, Ohranovich told the story: Jurich had returned home shortly after arriving from Australia and went to work for his father as a farmer and vintner. He never went near the sea again. Jurich married and after his father's death took over the farm and vineyard. Jurich died a natural death in his old age, and his only son, Nikola, took over the farm. Nikola and his wife had three sons, the oldest named Ivan after his grandfather.

Tragedy struck the family in 1943. Ivan Jurich was a young

Ivan Jurich, co-survivor—a photograph from Baccich's records

man in his twenties when the Germans arrived in Korčula. There was no resistance, but everyone wanted to see the soldiers. When the German troops assembled in the town square adjacent to the waterfront, the commander had three men from the crowd brought before him. He then had his men bind the three men

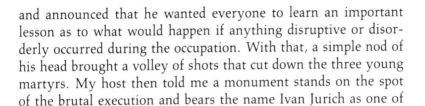

and announced that he wanted everyone to learn an important lesson as to what would happen if anything disruptive or disorderly occurred during the occupation. With that, a simple nod of his head brought a volley of shots that cut down the three young martyrs. My host then told me a monument stands on the spot of the brutal execution and bears the name Ivan Jurich as one of the victims.

By now I was curious about this articulate man who lived in such a small town and yet had such a sense of history. I asked him about the paintings and photographs on the walls. When I asked who were the two men in a photograph with Winston Churchill, I learned one was the Lord Mayor of London; the other, who was receiving a military decoration, was Marko Ohranovich, admiral in the Yugoslav Navy during World War II! His bravery and leadership succeeded in getting most of the Yugoslav fleet out of the Adriatic, and the Mediterranean, just before the Germans advanced. The fleet regrouped in Great Britain and served in North Atlantic convoy patrols with the British. Another photo showed the admiral with his old friend and admirer Josip Broz, better known as Tito.

Before leaving, I learned that Jurich's other two grandsons are successful wine merchants on the peninsula and that Jurich's nephew, ninety years old and blind, lives in Oskorušno. "This very day," said Ohranovich, "I will visit him to tell him about the wonderful experience I had with a man who came all the way from America to learn about his uncle Ivan Jurich, the friend and companion of his own grandfather, Miho Baccich."

The next day found me back in Korčula turning my attention from Jurich to Baccich, whose forebears had settled on that beautiful island centuries ago. I wanted to learn more about my ancestors on both sides of my grandfather's family. I was able to trace the paternal line back eleven generations to the sixteenth century. The most common vocation of the family was seafaring and shipbuilding. I originally thought Baccich's Uncle Nikola, the owner of the *Stefano*, was the first family member so employed. But I learned Baccich's grandfather, Anton, had been a ship's captain, and several members of the family Baccich or Bačić (and Bacetich, the diminutive of the family name) were prominent owners of oceangoing fleets in the sixteenth century.[1]

When Baccich began his life in America, it was in maritime-related occupations. His first job was working with a fellow countryman provisioning ships in the port of New Orleans. He took over the business several years later and married his former employer's daughter, Angelina. His family grew rapidly. By 1900, after thirteen years of marriage, he had seven children. His mother-in-law, Nina (née Vucassovich), lived with the family and helped with the children.

Baccich's second child, a daughter, was born on October 27, 1890, the fifteenth anniversary of his shipwreck. This remarkable coincidence caused him to commemorate the event further by initially naming the new baby girl Australia. However, his wife quickly set about to suggest a more appropriate alternative. Being a language scholar, she came up with an original name from the Greek—Euxenia—which roughly means "hospitality." More literally, it means "high [regard for] the stranger" (*eu-xenos*). The name was to remind the family of the lifesaving care bestowed on their husband and father, the stranger, by the people of the distant land.

The child lived up to her unusual name. She was my mother, to whose memory I have dedicated this book. The name has since been passed down to three generations.

Nine years later, on the twenty-fourth anniversary of the shipwreck, October 27, 1899, Baccich's youngest child, Anna, was born. (She is alive as of this writing.) This second event has caused me to wonder if the timing really was coincidence!

By 1905, Baccich had outgrown the store on the waterfront and was a partner in a three-man firm—Mueller, Baccich, and Clement, shipping agents—in the middle of the city's business district. He was still bound to the commerce of the sea, but by now a new opportunity was emerging.

For generations, it had been the family's tradition to be involved in the prosperous industry of the times. The principal industry of America at the turn of the century was not the sea but the land, and in keeping with the spirit of his upbringing, he chose his new career in real estate development, to be sure of his place in time to come.

A marked parallel between the lives of Baccich and his somewhat older rescuer, Charles Tuckey, was evident when the pair ex-

The Baccich family, 1910. Left to right: Euxenia, Miho Baccich, Eunice and Ida (standing), Anna (seated), George, Angelina Cietcovich Baccich, Lydia, and Hilda. Two of Baccich's daughters were born on October 27, the date of the fateful shipwreck: Euxenia (1890) and Anna (1899), the fifteenth and twenty-fourth anniversaries

changed letters in 1894. Baccich wrote first on January 9, and said in part:

> . . . I have always remembered you as a saviour, and I justly consider that it is owing to you that I am still in the land of the living. I consider you a second father, very dear to me . . . Your picture is always with me, and is kept in a prominent place in my family . . .

Tuckey replied on March 5:

> I am very glad to hear of you after so many years' absence. The mayor of Fremantle received a letter from you inquiring about me. I met him away from home and you may imagine my surprise and pleasure when I got home and found a letter for myself from you.

You wish to know how I am getting on. I am in business in a fish and fruit preserving factory and a small store which I started in September 1880 . . .

I am not now as when you saw me a single man. I have a wife and eight (8) children. I have quite given up sea-faring. Dear friend, I am pleased to tell you that I received a very nice gold watch from the Austro-Hungarian government on the representation by Lloyd's agent of your rescue which I prize very much.[†] Do you know where Giovanni Jurich is, who was saved with you . . .

Although apparently the reply was not yet to hand, Baccich wrote again on April 14 and enclosed a photograph of himself which presented to its recipient a man of thirty-four very much changed from the youth he had known. Tuckey replied on June 26:

. . . I can assure you I have often thought of you and spoken of the way our little cutter was driven back to the N.W. Cape by the strong winds to your rescue . . . When here you spoke of getting a pamphlet printed of your adventures on the N.W. Cape, and through not receiving a copy of that, it was with great surprise and pleasure that I received your letters . . . Dear Friend, I cannot express my thankfulness for your gratitude . . .

Charles Tuckey was in comfortable circumstances when he died in 1912 at the age of sixty-five. But, though it progressed steadily all along, it was to be another fifty years before Mandurah began to experience a boom in real estate which has brought its population to some twenty-five thousand today. It still has a Tuckey's Store on the original site and it has long had a Tuckey Street. Today the Tuckey family is large and well known in Western

[†] The gold watch is now held by the Royal Western Australian Historical Society. The inscription is in the Hungarian language, and this reflects the fact that Fiume (Rijeka), where the *Stefano* was registered, was the one port of the kingdom of Hungary; the rest of Dalmatia southward was governed as a province of the empire of Austria. Rijeka and Dalmatia are now incorporated in the republic of Croatia.

Australia, and indeed Wilson Tuckey, M.P., is prominent in national politics.[‡] I was fortunate to meet Captain Tuckey's last surviving son, Roy, in 1983; he was then ninety years old and I was pleased he remembered his father's tales about rescuing my grandfather.

I was sorry to find a sadder conclusion to the career of Captain Vincent, who had been such a good friend to the two stranded lads in 1876. On January 24, 1879, he was in command of his seventy-foot schooner *Rosette*, with women and children among its passengers, when he was obliged to anchor near Rosemary Island, fifty-six miles off Tien Tsin, in hope of riding out a fierce cyclone. The ship foundered in three fathoms, and there were no survivors. In 1987, I had the pleasure of meeting his granddaughter, Monica, who lives in Fremantle, and she kindly provided me with the photograph of Captain Vincent with his wife and children.

Baccich's first venture in the real estate business was with a partner of French descent, R.E.E. du Montluzin. Their major success was the first large subdivision carried out in New Orleans, and it extended the city boundaries north and eastward for a considerable distance. At that time the city was surrounded by water—the Mississippi River on one side, the large coastal Lake Pontchartrain on the other, and low swampland along the rest of the boundaries. The new development was called Gentilly Terrace, and "Terrace" was a significant part of the name. Most of the land available for new construction in the early 1900s was flooded by frequent rains and high tidal water from the lake. Baccich was able to buy large tracts of such land at low prices. Each building lot was filled with a terrace of earth hauled from distant highlands to provide a foundation for houses about four feet above the street level. Rains and floods would periodically cover the streets, but the houses were untouched, and the streets were back to normal in a day or two. A city street was named after Baccich in recognition of these

[‡] Charles Tuckey and his brother John, another sea captain, had a total of ten sons, and the surname continued in fourteen grandsons. Although Baccich and Jurich had only one son each, their grandsons succeeded in keeping the family name alive.

Mandurah 26 June 1894

My Dear Freind

       I have just received your second letter dated 14 April and we are very pleased receiving it with your picture Enclosed which is very good, I have one which you gave me 18 years ago and there is decidedly a great change.

I can assure you I have often thought of you and spoken of the way our little cutter was driven back to the N W Cape by the strong winds to your rescue, if you do not recollect I will relate the whole circumstances in future letters

When here you spoke of getting a pamphlet printed of your adventures on the N W Cape and through not receiving a copy of that, it was with great surprise and pleasure that I received your letters

Dear Freend I cannot Express my thankfulness for your gratitude and Kindness, and you may rest-assured you will never be forgotten by me, when I receive an answer to my letter registered to you last March I will send you my photo also one of my Father and mother taken at their golden wedding which was

Letter from Tuckey to Baccich, 1894

accomplishments. The partnership flourished for years; in 1924 Baccich sold his valuable interest to his partner. He had started another firm with his son in 1920.

    The firm and the real estate business in general prospered in the economic boom of the mid-1920s. The Great Depression that began in 1929 had an especially severe effect on real estate, and this was to last over twelve years, until World War II revitalized the industry.

    During his first ten years in America, Baccich had invested in gold-mining stocks. They all proved worthless and were perhaps

kept up on the 7th Dec 1891   they are still
living and well at the age of 78 and 72 —
years respectively
There are no photographers in mandurah
those in Fremantle are the nearest we have
(40 miles distance)
let me know how your family are
I shall always be glad to hear from you
and when I find you receive my letters safely
I will let you know my circumstances.
are there any machine manufactories in your
town if so will you kindly endeavour to
get particulars and cost of a machine for
fastining the Ends on round tins. without
Solder I have heard of the machine and
Seen the tins if I can get one of these
machines i believe it will answer for one
pound Fish tins and be a great Saving.

with best wishes from
your Sincear Freend

C. Tuckey

fraudulent ventures; but a few years after these investments
failed, he was again speculating, this time buying shares of stock
in the Panama Canal Company—*not* the successful undertaking
by the U.S. government but the quite unsuccessful attempt made
by the French company in northern Panama from 1888 to 1904.
Perhaps the unclipped coupons on the bonds left to me might
have value to a collector someday, but nothing more.

In the latter part of 1934, Grandfather, at age seventy-five, was
interviewed by a journalist from Zagreb, the capital of Croatia.
He was visiting America to learn more about the seafaring men
from the Dalmatian coast who had emigrated successfully all over

the world. Along with all his achievements in America, the thing Baccich spoke about most during the interview was his shipwreck experiences. The concluding lines of that interview are worth repeating. "Of course, I would rather be in my beloved Dubrovnik, but life is not always what one wishes. Life is an eternal compromise. But anyhow, I am at peace here. I am grateful; I have six daughters and one son. He runs my business and I rest, read, and wait by myself (my wife passed away ten long years ago). It is a long, long journey that I have traveled from 1859 till now."[2] A year later, in December 1935, the journey ended. His young years had been filled with excitement, adventure, and success. Well educated in an era when few were so fortunate, he was competent in five languages when he was but twenty years old, and was captain on the high seas at twenty-one. He proved brave and strong enough to survive both a tragic shipwreck and the Great Depression. He was a good, beloved husband and father, and the only grandparent I ever knew.

NOTES

Introduction
1. Josip Luetić, "Contributions of the Southern Dalmatian Coast to the International Maritime Trade of the Republic of Dubrovnik, 1597–1807," *Naše More* 1–2 (1985), 47–68.
Mato Petrović, ed., *12 Vjekova Bokeljske Mornarice* [12 Centuries of the Bay of Kotor's Merchant Marine] (Belgrade: Monos, 1972).

2. J.H.M. Honniball, "The Tuckeys of Mandurah," *Early Days (Journal of the Royal Western Australian Historical Society)* 5, part 8 (1961), 7–50.

3. Neven Smoje, "Shipwrecked on the North-West Coast," in *Early Days* 8, part 2 (1978), 35–47.

Epigraph
1. Leslie Marchant, *France Australe* (Perth: Artlook, 1982).

Chapter 3
1. G. and K. J. Henderson, *Unfinished Voyages: Western Australian Shipwrecks 1851–1880* (Nedlands: University of Western Australia Press, 1988).

Chapter 4
1. Carter's early diaries have been published under the title *No Sundays in the Bush: An English Jackeroo in Western Australia 1887–1889*

(Melbourne: Lothian, 1987), and the quotation above appears on page 123. See also Freda Vines, "Thomas Carter, Ornithologist," *Early Days* 6, part 7 (1968), 7–21.

Chapter 6

1. Accounts of cannibalism in Western Australia are varied and sometimes contradictory. See also:

   E. J. Stormon, ed., *The Salvado Memoirs* (Nedlands: University of Western Australia Press, 1977).

   R. M. and C. A. Berndt, *The World of the First Australians* (Sydney: Ure Smith, 1964).

   P. J. Bridge, ed., *Cannibalism in Australia* (Carlisle: Hesperian Press, in preparation).

Epilogue

1. Josip Luetić, "The Merchant Fleet, Ship Owners, and Captains of Korčula," *Naše More* 6 (1983), 187–94.

2. L. M. Pejovic, *Yugoslavs in the South U.S.A.* (New Orleans: Dameron-Pierson, 1935).

ABORIGINAL–ENGLISH–
ITALIAN GLOSSARY

This is a listing of words and phrases used by the Aborigines which Baccich and Jurich learned and incorporated in the story they recounted, although it is not quite exhaustive of all such words in the text. It is a combination of the collection as compiled by Stjepan Skurla (Aboriginal/ Italian) and of the 1920 translation (Aboriginal/English). There may be some benefit for linguistic studies in this amalgamation of the two sources and also in the preservation of the listing's original arrangement of the words in groupings. There are a few oddities in it, some of them caused by inconsistencies in the two manuscripts and by difficulties in interpreting the handwriting. Some of the words, e.g., *Parue*— faraway—are corruptions of English words which the natives had acquired in their limited contact with the settlers and pearlers. Variant English meanings that have now been added are distinguished by italics.

Giunovagnabari	Name of tribe's deity		Nome di divinità	
Bengo	Proper noun—masc.		Nome proprio—masch.	
Cagiaro	"	"	"	"
Cialli (corruption)	"	" *Charlie*	"	"
Cincigo	"	"	"	"
Gjaki, Giachi	"	" *Jacky*	"	"
Gjimmi, Gimmi	"	" *Jimmy*	"	"
Igranne, Igrane	"	"	"	"

Michi	"	" *Micky*	"	"
Naman	"	"	"	"
Tairo	"	"	"	"
Tondogoro	"	"	"	"
Nili	"	—fem. *Nellie?*	"	—fem.
Sandi	———	*Sandy*	——	
Tobi	———	*Toby*	——	

Bundegi	Name of locality	Nome di una località, forse dal verbo bundaj
Caracara	Perth (city), *Karrakatta (Perth)*	Perth (città)
Pulimandur	Fremantle (city)	id.
Cincin	Tiensin (city), *Tien Tsin*	Tiensin (città)
Cinaman	Chinaman	Cinese
Vac-balla	A white man, *a white fellow*	Uomo bianco
Bulac-balla	A black man, *a black fellow*	Uomo negro
Pichinini	A boy, *piccaninny*	Ragazzo
*Curi	A youth between 16 and 20	Giovane dai 16–20 anni
Cominini	Married women	Donne sposate
Kughi	A cook	Cuoco (corr. dall'Ing.)
Ta	Mouth	Bocca
Tulla	Eyes	Occhi
Najengolo	Nose	Naso
Cina	Sole of foot	Pianta
Poleo	Calf of leg	Polpaccio

* *Curi* in the text appears to refer to a younger child.

Gundum-balla	Male organs, *? penis fellow*	Membro virile
Vandi	Male organs, *? testicles*	id.
Be	Fish	Pesce
Jamina, janina	Dugong	Pesce dugon
Mulla	Birds	Uccelli
Tataruga	A turtle or a tortoise	Tartaruga (testuggini)
Vangia	Dog	Cane
Cocongiai	Goat	Capra
Bilgura	Intestines of fish	Interiore del pesce
Manda vangi, manda vanchi	Crabs and crayfish	Granchi
Birra	Shell	Conchiglia
Cembo	Egg	Uova
Pinoro	Fire	Fuoco
Calla	Wood	Legna
Milli milli	Paper	Carta
Bulava	Flour	Farina
Ciugga	Sugar	Zucchero
Turaggi	Rice	Riso
Thie	Tea	Tè
Coconagi	Coconuts	Cocco
Nurgan	Fat	Grasso
Ianda	Sun	Sole
Villara	Stars or moon	Stelle o luna
Iango	Rain	Pioggia
Babba	Water	Acqua
Buria	Sea	Mare

Denki	Skiff, yawl, *dinghy*	Barca, guzzo
Tanic-balla	Ship, *ship fellow*	Bastimento
Trala	A sail	Vela
Majabulo	Canoe	Piroga
Culgo–Manda	———	Ferro–Sasso
Culgo	Iron	———
Manda	Log of wood, *? stone*	———
Paura (corruption)	Gunpowder	Polvere da sparo
Ciumberi	Iron weapons	Armi di ferro
Tanta	Trousers	Pantaloni
Ciar	Shirt	Camicia
Cianguru, Ciangura	Hat	Cappello
Ciucigo	Shoes	Scarpe
Niril (corruption)	Needles	Aghi
Galle	An Australian weapon	Certa arme austr.
Bellara	An Australian spear	Una specia di lancia
Bellara manno	An Australian weapon	Un arme degli indigeni
Bemanno	An Australian fishing spear	Lancia per pescare
Vario	A vine	Vigna
Puliman	Butter	Burro
Island (Eng.)	Island	Isola (dall'Ing.)
To morning (Eng.)	Tomorrow morning	Domani mattina
Oggin, Oggui	I, me	Io, me
Niengo	You	Voi

Virago	Sick	Ammalato
Ulmo	—— Old	Vecchio
Gamogo	Starving	Affamato
Birida	Thirsty	Assetato
Vabba	Good	Buono
Mira vabba	Bad, *no good*	Cattivo
Cungiri	One	Uno
Gudara	Two	Due
Vrai	From two to ten	Da 2 a 10
Brr	From ten on	Dal 10 in avanti
Mamma	Very much	Molto
Ciullu	Very many	Molto
Arima	To die	Morire
Bundaj	Bathe in the sea	Bagnare nel mare
Bagaj	To shipwreck	Naufragare
Bagialgo	To eat and drink	Mangiare e bere
Bambaj	To sleep	Dormire
Bolue	To row	Vogare
Cagliadaga	To kiss	Baciare
Cinci-cinci	To divide, *to share*	Dividere
Dadalgo	To take	Prendere
Daghi, dagi	To come	Venire
Gogoj	To return	Venire, ritornare
Galbaj	To arise	Alzare
Tungoro	To give	Dare
Jurogaja	To approach	Avvicinare
Komin (corruption)	To come	Venire
Nagaru	To see, to observe	Vedere, osservare
Pignari	To quarrel	Baruffare, disputare
Tantargoria	To sit down	Sedere

Vagaj	To go	Andare
Voteri	To search	Cercare
Minara	In a short while	Fra breve
Parue	Far, distant, *faraway*	Lontano
Muriandi	Quick	Presto
Iggiala	Immediately	Subito
Vangi	Where	Dove
Bullura	Before, ahead	Avanti
Nulla	Here	Qui
Villa	How	Come
Mira	No	Non
Go	Ola! *Hello!* (exclam.)	Ola
Kaciujamoro, Caciugliamoru	Poor fellow "	Poveretto! (esclam.)
Caibiri	Unfortunate me "	Me disgraziata! "
Cungeri	Oh the devil! "	Oh diavolo! "
Inagoin	So much	Tanto
Noru volu	What do you want?	Che cosa volete?
Tanic-balla bagaj	The ship is wrecked	Il bastimento ha naufragato
Calla voteri	To gather wood	Raccogliere legna
Be voteri	To go fishing	Pescare
Cinci mamma	Very fat	Molto grasso
Tungoro aggin	Give me	Date a me
Ianda budaj	The sun is setting	Il sole tramonta
Vangi bambaj	Where will we sleep?	Dove dormiremo?
Babba birida	He is thirsty	Ha sete
Cinci-cinci bagialgo	Let us divide the food	Dividiamo il cibo

Niengo gamogo	You are hungry	Voi avete fame
Niengo mamma gamogo	You are very hungry	Voi avete molto fame
Niengo mira bagialgo	You will not eat	Voi non mangerete
Niengo babba dirido	You are thirsty	Voi avete sete
Tungoro bagialgo babba	Give me a drink of water	Dammi a bever acqua
Vangi vagaj	Where are you going?	Dove vai?
Minara jongo gogaj	It will rain soon	Fra breve verra la pioggia
Cir irui	To satisfy nature's demands, to void	Orinare, liberare l'intestino (evacuare)
Pignari cominini	Women are mean	Il donne sono baruffante
Tendi vangiu geri	An ugly word, a curse	Differente bestemmie
Tendi balan geri	" "	" "
Tendi duga	" "	" "
Paur paur gutari Puhur cerima Moli gumagura	The evening song or verses which had never been understood	Tre versi che usano cantare di sera

Additionally, the original manuscript reports that the Aborigines called Baccich *Mir* in corruption of his Christian name Miho, and Jurich became *Tigone* in place of Ivan.

INDEX
Page numbers in italics refer to illustrations